D1006483

ELECTILE DYSFUNCTION

Electile
Dysfunction

*A Guide for
Unaroused Voters*

ALAN DERSHOWITZ

RosettaBooks®

NEW YORK 2016

First edition published 2016 by RosettaBooks
Jacket design by Corina Lupp
Typography by Jay McNair

Library of Congress Control Number: 2016950026
ISBN-13 (Hardcover): 978-0-7953-5021-4
ISBN-13 (EPUB): 978-0-7953-5020-7

Printed in the USA

This book is lovingly dedicated to
my great-nieces and -nephews,
Zara, Mars, Austin, and Marley—
future voters (and perhaps office-holders)
who will remedy our current electile dysfunction

Contents

INTRODUCTION
"Everybody Sucks 2016"

The 2016 presidential election—the most bizarre in my lifetime—may well be decided not by which candidate is liked more than the other, but rather by which is disliked less. Polls show that a majority of Americans have unfavorable opinions of both Donald Trump and Hillary Clinton and would strongly consider supporting a third-party candidate. Indeed, an Associated Press poll taken just before the nominating conventions found that "81 percent of Americans say they would feel afraid following the election of one of the two politicians," and 25 percent said, "It doesn't matter who wins. They're scared of both."[1] This antagonism is apparently so widespread that an online store is selling bumper stickers, shirts, signs, and other paraphernalia with the logo EVERYBODY SUCKS 2016.

One comment writer to the *New York Times* explained that he wouldn't vote for Trump or Clinton because, he said: "I'm resigned to having a terrible president starting next January, but there is no way I'll be responsible for electing him or her."[2] Still more voters who plan to cast a ballot will be voting *against*, not *for* one of the candidates:

"Three-quarters of voters say their selection would be motivated more by a desire to keep either Trump or Clinton out of the Oval Office" than by a desire to see their own candidate elected.[3]

Rarely have both candidates, both parties, and both houses of Congress been viewed so unfavorably[4] by the voting public. Voters are angry, frustrated, and resentful, and with good reason: over the past several years, Congress has been incapable of passing even the most uncontroversial legislation, much less taking meaningful steps to address some of the serious economic and social problems facing our nation. This has resulted in the president taking constitutionally questionable steps, such as executive orders on immigration and on environmental regulations, which the courts have struck down. The result has been gridlock and stalemate.

There is frustration among working-class people whose take-home pay has not kept pace with those at the top of the economic pyramid, especially on Wall Street. There is anger among people of color regarding the symptoms of what they believe is structural racism manifested in high unemployment, high rates of imprisonment, and increasingly visible police bias. There is disappointment over our inability to deal rationally with what many view as a crisis regarding our immigration policy. And there is emotional fury—some rational, some not—about the state of our country and the world. Throughout history, radical left-wing extremists, as well as reactionary right-wing extremists, have exploited popular grievances such as these to their political advantage. This dangerous phenomenon is threatening many countries around the world today. It is also impacting the current election here at home.

The Shrinking Center

In the kind of political environment we are now experiencing, campaigns tend to emphasize the negative over the positive, the unfavorable over the favorable, and the downsides over the upsides. Voters look to simple-minded panaceas, to change for change's sake, to revolution over evolution, to disruptive violence—and to extremes on both sides of the political spectrum. Hence the success of Donald Trump and the unexpected strength of Bernie Sanders—both of whom ran against more centrist, establishment candidates. The actress and Sanders surrogate Susan Sarandon explained why, in her view, "outsiders like Sanders and Trump have become so popular":

> "A lot of people felt disenfranchised. A lot of people are working so hard and getting nowhere. A lot of people are sick with politics the way it is... Bernie and Trump spoke to those people ...." Then she added, "It's like the dark and the light ... so will some of those people go over to the dark side ... I don't know, people are angry."[5]

Although Hillary Clinton, herself a more centrist candidate, eventually won the Democratic nomination, she did so by moving away from the center and adopting some of Sanders's left-wing positions and populist political rhetoric. Even after securing the nomination, she continued to drift leftward in an effort to secure the support of Sanderistas, who threatened to stay home or vote for Jill Stein of the hard-left Green Party. This is how Sarandon put it: "I'm waiting to be seduced. I'm waiting to be convinced.[6] ... I'm waiting to hear something that speaks to me.... I'm not buying [Clinton] until she offers me something."[7]

Some Sanders supporters have even threatened to vote for Trump over Clinton, whom they regard as too centrist. As the journalist Christopher Ketcham—another prominent Sanders surrogate—put it: "I'd rather see the empire burn to the ground under Trump, opening up at least the possibility of radical change, than cruise on autopilot under Clinton."[8]

Clinton's acceptance speech incorporated some of Sanders's rhetoric and policies. But there is the fear that if Clinton tries too hard to seduce Sarandon and her fellow "Bernie or bust" radicals—if she moves too far away from the center—she could lose the support of traditional elements of the Democratic coalition who voted for candidates like Kerry and Obama but will not vote for Clinton if they perceive her to have moved away from them.

In the process of trying to secure the votes of such die-hard Sanders supporters, Clinton may well lose the votes of some centrist Republicans who were reluctant to vote for Trump and were considering voting for Clinton but may now end up voting for the Trump. As one Republican friend put it to me: "If the choice is between a kooky Republican and a reasonable Democrat, I will probably hold my nose and vote Democrat. But if the choice is between a kooky Republican and a kooky Democrat, hey, I might as well stick to my own Republican kook."

The current move away from the center and toward extremes—from centrist liberalism and moderate conservatism toward an ill-defined radical populism—is occurring in varying degrees around the globe, and it is a dangerous trend that threatens the stability of America and the world. The Brexit vote in Great Britain, the increasing power of both the hard right and hard left in many

European countries, the growing influence of Islamic extremism within Muslim communities, the call for violence among some American radicals—both left and right—all point in a similar direction.

This trend has been replicated on university campuses around the world—campuses that train future leaders and voters. Indeed, students of both the hard left and the fundamentalist right seem less committed to classic academic values such as freedom of speech and the right of teachers to discuss difficult issues, and are increasingly obsessed with political correctness and suppression of dissenting or offensive voices.

The Global Movement Toward Extremes

Among the greatest dangers confronting the world today is the movement away from the centrist politics that have characterized most democracies over the past several decades and toward the extremes of both left and right. History has demonstrated that the growing influence of extremism on either side of the political spectrum stimulates the growth of extremism on the other side. The move toward hard-left radicalism provokes movement toward hard-right radicalism, and vice versa. The hard right is becoming more empowered in Poland, Slovakia, and Greece, and authoritarian leaders control Russia, Turkey, Belarus, and Hungary. The hard left has increased its influence in universities and labor unions and within some traditionally centrist liberal political parties, such as Labour in Great Britain and the Democrats in the United States. Populism is pushing toward extremes on both ends of the political spectrum. And extremism at one end tends to provoke extremism on the other end, as we are now witnessing. The growth of both extremes weakens the liberal and conservative centers and moves the world away from stability, rationality, tolerance, and nuance—and toward demagoguery, simple-mindedness, xenophobia, and intolerance.

Following the British vote to leave the European Union —which occurred despite the opposition of both major political parties in the UK—former prime minister Tony Blair, himself a centrist liberal, warned that instability will only increase unless the center can

> regain its political traction, rediscover its capacity to analyze the problems we all face and find solutions that rise above the populist anger.... If we do not succeed in beating back the far left and far right before they take the nations of Europe on this reckless experiment, it will end the way such rash action always does in history: at best, in disillusion; at worst, in rancorous division. The center must hold.

Similarly, the French philosopher Bernard-Henri Lévy saw the Brexit vote as a "victory of the hard right over the moderate right, and the radical over the liberal left."

Time and time again, history has demonstrated that extremism in politics—whether right, left, or both—is dangerous to the world. Extremists brook no dissent because they "know" the "truth." We often forget that the benign-sounding term "political correctness" originated under Stalin, who murdered political dissenters, artists, musicians, and others who deviated from the politically correct line. Extremists begin by banning and burning books, and they end by banning and burning people.

The enemy of the hard left is not the hard right, because extremes develop symbiotic relationships with each other. The real enemies of the radical left are centrist liberals, just as the real enemies of the reactionary right are centrist conservatives.

It is these centrists, both liberal and conservative, who are being squeezed by the extremes. It is centrism itself—with its stability, its willingness to compromise, its tolerance for divergent views, and its capacity to govern effectively if not perfectly—that is currently in the crosshairs of populist extremism.

We are seeing that disturbing phenomenon all over the world. It must not be allowed to take root here.

The Importance of the 2016 Election

In terms of stability of the world and of our nation, the 2016 presidential election may be among the most important in generations. Many voters cannot vote for a destabilizing and unpredictable candidate like Donald Trump, or for a Republican Party that opposes the reproductive rights of women, the right of gays to marry, the right of citizens to health care, and other extreme Republican policies, such as opposition to effective gun control. But many voters also distrust Hillary Clinton and are wary of the foreign policy of the Democratic Party, especially with regard to terrorism and the Middle East. They are particularly concerned about the efforts of the left wing of the Democratic Party to weaken our nation's support for

Israel. Centrist Democrats are also wary of hard-left "identity politics" that emphasize group rights over individual rights. Moderate Republicans are equally wary of Trump's emphasis on group wrongs that tends to lump together "the Mexicans," "the blacks," "the gays," and other groups of individuals based on their ethnicity, gender, or sexual orientation.

The result of this movement toward extremes has been a weakening of the center and confusion among many voters, who don't like the choices currently on the ballot. They reject what they see as the growing influence of the hard left within the Democratic Party—especially but not exclusively with regard to foreign policy and identity politics—and they cannot accept the religiously motivated domestic policies of the Republican hard right. Many centrists—both Democrats and Republicans alike—do not feel they now have a comfortable home in either party, and they are not aroused by either candidate.

Over the past months, I have been making these observations in my speeches and public appearances. Invariably, dozens of people come up and say, "That's me! I, too, am a domestic liberal who supports Israel and a more muscular foreign policy. I'm worried about what is happening on university campuses, with left-wing suppression of speech. I'm not sure I can vote for Democrats who demonize Israel and pander to hard-left identity politics, but I don't think that I can vote for Republicans who are anti–gay rights, women's rights, and other liberal programs. What should I do?"

Hence this book. It describes the political dysfunction and the dilemma faced by centrist voters who are not aroused by either candidate or party, and it proposes constructive ways to deal with it.

In the chapters to come, I will analyze how politically perplexed citizens, who are torn between liberal domestic values that incline them to support Democratic candidates, and foreign policy values that might incline them to support Republican candidates, might think about this conflict. As a teacher for half a century, I never told my students what values to accept or which candidates to support. I always helped guide them to conclusions based on their own sets of values. I will try to do the same in this book. I will not tell readers whether to support Democratic or Republican candidates. Instead I will try to sort out both the domestic and foreign policy values that each reader might possess. I will then set out a process for assessing these values and prioritizing them.

My goal is to have each reader think for her or himself about the comparative strength of each of their values and how they might prioritize them in an effort to come to rational conclusions regarding candidates and political parties. I will not try to hide my personal views as to which of the current presidential candidates I believe will do a better job of moving us toward centrist liberalism. But nor will I use this book as an explicit campaign screed for or against Hillary Clinton or Donald Trump. Some readers will analyze their values and priorities in a manner that will make them vote for Democratic candidates while others will be inclined to vote for Republicans. That is as it should be in a democracy.

It is my hope that no one will stay home in this most important of presidential elections. Democracy requires choice, even if it is between candidates who do not arouse positive passions.

1

The Causes of the Dysfunction

When I came of age in the 1950s and 1960s, the political choices facing families like mine were rather simple. The Democrats were the liberals who supported the center-left causes of the day. To be sure, there was the Dixiecrat wing of the Democratic Party that was obstructionist on issues of racial equality. But the Democrats for whom we voted—Adlai Stevenson, John Kennedy, Lyndon Johnson, Hubert Humphrey, and Robert Kennedy—supported desegregation and a variety of other liberal causes. They were more likely to oppose capital punishment, McCarthyism, military adventurism, and other conservative agenda items that were supported by most Republicans. The Democrats were the defenders of New Deal social programs, of civil liberties, civil rights, and basic decency. To be sure, there were Republicans who leaned center left on some issues, such as Senator Jacob Javits and Nelson Rockefeller. But for the most part, the Democrats were the liberals and the

Republicans were the conservatives. The Democrats were the party of working people, the Republicans of the rich.

The Democrats were also more supportive of Israel than were the Republicans. President Truman was the first world leader to recognize Israel in 1948, while President Eisenhower was openly hostile to Israel in 1956, when, along with Great Britain and France, they invaded Egypt to secure freedom of passage through the Suez Canal. Among the strongest supporters of Israel in the Senate were Hubert Humphrey, Robert Kennedy, and other leaders of the liberal wing of the Democratic Party.

Though the divisions between the parties were not as stark as they are today—they actually worked together to enact civil rights and other reforms—for most centrist liberals the choice was clear: the Democrats were on our side, the good side, the liberal side. For most centrist conservatives the choice was also clear: the Republicans were on their side, the conservative side.

Oh, how things have changed over the past half century! The Democratic Party has been pushed farther left by the growing influence of radical activist organizations such as MoveOn, Occupy Wall Street, Code Pink, the National Lawyers Guild, and Black Lives Matter, as well as by leftward pressure from young voters, especially university students. This was manifested during the 2016 primary season by the surprising success of Bernie Sanders and the leftward push his voters gave Hillary Clinton.

On the Republican side, the influence of the religious right has all but destroyed the moderate wing of the party. There are few if any Rockefeller Republicans elected to public office today. For a Republican to win the intraparty primary in many, if not most, parts of the country, he or she must be anti–abortion rights, anti–gay rights, anti–gun control, and for religious freedom laws that endanger the separation of church and state. Even a committed, right-leaning centrist Republican like Eric Cantor, who was at the top of Republican House leadership, was deemed too moderate and could not withstand a primary challenge from a hard-right Tea Party extremist.

The political climate today seems more polarized than at any point in my lifetime.

There are several distinct issues that have moved the Democratic Party away from centrist liberalism and the Republican Party away from centrist conservatism. But the movements to the extreme left and extreme right that have created so much discomfort among centrists of both parties transcend particular issues. They go to the heart and soul of the Democratic and Republican parties. Much has already been written about the radicalization of the Republican Party by the religious right and tea partiers. In the coming pages, I will focus primarily on the growing radicalization of the Democratic Party by the hard left. I will first address the specific issues related to this process and then the more general trends.

Identity Politics, Intersectionality, and Bigotry: From the Campus to the Future

The left wing of the Democratic Party, over the past several years, has moved in the direction of those "revolutionaries" of my generation who became radical professors and teaching assistants in many universities. Some of them have long preached a radical theory called intersectionality, which holds that all oppressed social groups are linked together in a common struggle against a colonialist, imperialist, patriarchal, and homophobic sociopolitical and economic order. America and Israel are the leading villains in this fictional narrative—they are the embodiments of this "oppressive" establishment.

The would-be revolutionaries encourage their adherents—and the perceived victims—to engage with the political process along lines of race, gender, ethnicity, and sexual preference. This form of identity politics prioritizes particular immutable characteristics over shared American values and leads to a double standard in both domestic and foreign policy that increases political polarization and erodes the principles of equality, civil liberties, and basic fairness. Centrist liberals reject the extremism of Occupy Wall Street, the simple-mindedness of Code Pink, the one-sidedness of the National Lawyers Guild, and the parochialism of Black Lives Matter. While we recognize the realities of structural racism in the United States, for us, black lives matter because all lives matter equally—and because we recognize that this has not always been accepted and implemented despite the principles embodied in our Declaration of Independence and the constitutional right to equal protection.*

In some respects, but not in others, the dilemma we currently confront is a variation on an old conflict

---

* One can, of course, support the *concept* of black lives mattering without necessarily supporting the organization Black Lives Matter, especially since many of its leaders and activists support objectionable concepts as well. Some people use the phrase "all lives matter" to undercut "black lives matter." That is not what I am trying to do. It's a tragedy that some activists in the organization insist on diluting its central message and thereby alienating many potential supporters.

between centrist liberals and hard-left radicals. Genuine liberals—who believe in tolerance, freedom of expression, and democratic values—have always been targeted by the radical left as traitors to the cause. The Mensheviks were the enemies of the Bolsheviks; the Roosevelt liberals were the enemies of the 1930s Communists; the NAACP and Martin Luther King Jr. were the enemies of Malcolm X and the Black Panthers; and President Obama is the enemy of Cornel West—a vocal supporter of Bernie Sanders who has refused to support Hillary Clinton—who has called Obama "the first niggerized president," a racial epithet that, if it were used by a white person, would forever disqualify him from being taken seriously.* Today's traditional centrist liberals are the enemies of the newly minted radicals on the hard left, just as traditional centrist conservatives—who want to keep government out of our bedrooms, doctors' offices, and churches—are the enemies of the newly empowered hard religious right.

This conflict between traditional centrist liberalism and contemporary hard-left radicalism is being played out on a micro level in universities around the world, and most recently on American campuses, including the Ivy League. I devoted half a century of my life to teaching at Harvard—with visiting stints at Stanford, Yale, NYU, and Hebrew University—and have spoken at dozens of universities in the US and around the world. I continue to monitor developments on campuses and to be involved in the defense of freedom of expression at universities. It is appalling to me that today's radical students are demanding

---

* West was also the enemy of Harvard's former president, the liberal Lawrence Summers, whom he called "the Ariel Sharon of higher education." Pam Belluck, "Defector Indignant at President of Harvard," *New York Times*, April 16, 2002.

restrictions on freedom of speech in the interest of "safe spaces," political correctness, "trigger warnings," and protections against microaggression and other forms of expression they deem offensive or insensitive to them or their paranoid partners in persecution. They insist that students and faculty members who disagree with their approach to racial, gender, and political issues be required to check their privilege and to undergo "sensitivity training."

My generation of Jewish, Italian, Irish, and other immigrant children had no privileges to check. We were struggling against the privileged aristocrats who imposed quotas on our opportunities for advancement. Civil rights activists of my generation fought to speak freely against the McCarthyite censorship that was then prevalent on university campuses, not to screen Halloween costumes for potentially offensive content.

My grandson, who is a student at Harvard and a member of the *Lampoon*, the Harvard humor magazine, attended the 2015 Harvard-Yale football game with a friend who held up a humorous sign that read, "Tackling is a microaggression." Some people laughed, but others berated them for their insensitivity toward minorities and accused them of a microaggression and of "politically incorrect behavior" that warranted discipline.

"It's a joke. That's what the *Lampoon* does. It makes fun of everything," replied my grandson.

"Well, it's not funny," insisted the political-correctness police.

A recent documentary entitled *Can We Take a Joke* concluded that "more efforts to muzzle comics are coming from the left than from the right."[1] When I was a student, censorship nearly always emanated from the right. Today's young censors and their like-minded professors are generally on the left. They believe they know the Truth and they see no need to be exposed to other perspectives, even humorous ones, especially if they might offend "protected" groups.

Liberals, on the other hand, understand that the quest for truth is a never-ending process. Ultimate truth, especially in the realm of politics, morality, law, or economics, is an illusory holy grail. It will never be found. Just as "the fight for liberty never stays won,"[2] so too the search for truth never ends. One truth begets others, with a great many falsehoods along the way. As the great Judge Learned Hand once put it: "The spirit of liberty is the spirit which is not too sure that it is right." And that spirit must welcome conflicting views, even deeply offensive ones, into the open marketplace of ideas. What John Stuart Mill warned about the dangers of censoring dissenters is particularly relevant to current efforts to stifle speech that offends hard leftists on campuses: "Teachers and learners go to sleep at their post, as soon as there is no enemy in the field."[3]

The hard-left enemies of liberty reject that marketplace, just as they reject liberalism itself as class-based privilege that they want to see checked. They have little tolerance for intellectual diversity while demanding racial and other forms of diversity that bring to campus more students and faculty who share their profiles. They disdain Israel and other Western democracies while refusing to criticize third-world tyrannies that reject the most basic human rights. They demand safe-space protections for themselves against microaggressions, but deny those same protections to Jewish supporters of Israel and to

Christians who seek to promote their faith on campus.

Anti-Israel zealots demand the inclusion of anti-Zionist and often anti-American agenda items on any list of "progressive" demands. They insist that you cannot be a true leftist on domestic issues without singling out Israel and demonizing the nation-state of the Jewish people for its alleged oppression of Palestinians.[4] The theory of intersectionality—which has no basis in history, current events, or logic—is deployed to justify the reverse racism and discrimination implicit in the Boycott, Divestment, and Sanctions (BDS) campaign that targets Israel, and Israel alone, for its imperfections while giving a pass to left-wing and Muslim repression.

Consider for example, Jill Stein, the Green Party environmentalist candidate for president, who recently declared her support for BDS against Israel in a lengthy statement where she called for "ending support for governments committing war crimes and massive human rights violations...." She proceeded to decry Israel as an apartheid state and to compare it to nations with undemocratic tyrannies that notoriously massacred civilians during the Arab Spring uprisings of 2011, and to Saudi Arabia, which engages in overt gender and religious apartheid.

Stein's endorsement of BDS follows a disturbing trend. In recent years, anti-Israel zealots have succeeded in hijacking left-wing agendas involving the environment, race, gender, economic inequality, and even animal rights. They claim that Jews and Zionists are the oppressors not only of the Palestinians, but also of environmentalists, gays, blacks, and other politically correct "identities."

There is, of course, both a logical and empirical inconsistency between identity politics, which claims that all racial, gender, and other identities are unique and must not be culturally expropriated by other identities, and intersectionality, which claims that there is commonality in the persecution of these identities. But neither logic nor facts seem to get in the way of the political agenda of the hard left.

The candidacy of Bernie Sanders helped to mainstream both identity politics and intersectionality into Democratic Party politics—indeed, many of his supporters were holding signs reading

INTERSECTIONALITY MATTERS

at the Democratic convention. Few of the Clinton delegates understood the term or realized it is often used as a code word for anti-American, anti-Israel, and even anti-Semitic bigotry. Sanders's surrogate, the radical public intellectual Cornel West, is a prominent theorist of identity politics and intersectionality and was appointed by Sanders as a delegate to the Democratic platform committee. In a foreword to Angela Davis's recent screed with the telling title *Freedom Is a Constant Struggle: Ferguson, Palestine, and the Foundations of a Movement*, West defines intersectionality as "a structural intellectual and political response to the dynamics of violence, white supremacy, patriarchy, state power, capitalist markets, and imperial policies." Not surprisingly, West has now refused to support Hillary Clinton and has instead endorsed Jill Stein and her hard-left Green Party.

Intersectionality is practiced by a wide range of so-called progressive groups, including many radical feminists and gay-rights activists, who refuse to condemn the sexism and homophobia in the Arab world while reserving their wrath for the imperfections of Israel. When confronted with Israel's excellent record on gay rights, they even go so far to accuse Israel of pinkwashing[5]—that is, using its record on gay rights to cover its policies with regard to Palestinians. This fits the classic definition of anti-Semitism under which Jews—and now their nation-state—can do no right: whatever *good* they do—give to charity, educate their children, become involved in politics or business, and now promote gay rights—must have an *evil* motive.

This bigoted nonsense on stilts is also believed by many members of the National Women's Studies Association. With no obvious connection to its main mission—the promotion of feminist teachings in education—the organization passed a resolution in support of the BDS movement, explaining, "One cannot call oneself a feminist and address inequalities and injustices without taking a stand on what is happening in Palestine." I guess one *can* call oneself a feminist without taking a stand on what is happening in Tibet, Iran, Turkey, Saudi Arabia, Syria, and other places where rape is employed as a weapon of war, where women are prohibited from voting, where gays are thrown off rooftops, where honor killings of women are encouraged, and where children are beheaded.

Similarly, the Native American and Indigenous Studies Association (NAISA) joined the BDS movement. In its statement, it encouraged all its members "to boycott Israeli academic institutions." Needless to say, NAISA never issued a similar boycott in order to end Turkey's occupation of Cyprus or China's occupation of Tibet. Israel, and Israel alone, is singled out, and Israeli academics, regardless of their individual views, are being subjected to collective punishment. Equally shameful, the Association for Asian American Studies has approved a resolution to support the BDS movement. Its president likened the boycott to those levied against South African universities during the apartheid era and argued that the goal of the boycott is to "discourage partnerships with Israeli academic institutions, whether they're curriculum partnerships or study abroad partnerships, because that would be becoming complicit with the discriminatory practices of Israeli institutions and [to encourage] faculty, staff, and students to forge alliances with Palestinian faculty and Palestinian students who now have so much difficulty engaging in conversations with scholars from the rest of the world." This ignores the fact that Palestinians and Arabs, even those who are viciously anti-Israel, such as the BDS leader Omar Barghouti, can freely study at Israeli universities, while Israeli Jews, even if they are pro-Palestinian, are routinely banned from Palestinian universities.[6] Again, facts matter little to these close-minded academics.

Intersectionality also explains why some prominent Black Lives Matters activists, who were instrumental in the Sanders campaign, have aligned themselves against Israel. In a recent statement, one thousand black activists, including prominent Sanders supporters, declared:

> US and Israeli officials and media criminalize our existence, portray violence against us as "isolated incidents," and call our resistance "illegitimate" or "terrorism." These narratives ignore decades and centuries of anti-Palestinian and anti-Black violence that have always been at the core of Israel and the US.... These issues call for unified action against anti-Blackness, white supremacy, and Zionism.[7]

The platform released on August 1, 2016, by more than 60 organizations affiliated with the Black Lives Matter movement characterized Israel as "an apartheid state" and accused it of committing "genocide"[8]—a blood libel against the nation-state of the Jewish people that is reminiscent of false accusations leveled against the Jewish people for centuries. Of all countries in the world with human rights issues, only Israel was singled out for such mendacious condemnation.

These demonstrably false accusations against a foreign country not only alienate supporters here at home, they weaken the credibility of Black Lives Matter when it comes to police abuses against African-Americans. But the drafters of this bigoted platform plank seem willing to endanger their central mission in order to pander to intersectionalist extremists.

An even more extreme statement by Malik Zulu Shabazz, the national president of Black Lawyers for Justice, which has been associated with Black Lives Matter, "suggested killing all Zionists in Israel, including their 'old ladies' and 'little babies.'"* He has demanded that Jews and

---

* John Eligon and Frances Robles, "Amid Push to Curb Police Abuse, Some Act on Fringe," *New York Times*, July 23, 2016. Nor has Shabazz limited his hateful vitriol to Zionists. He blamed Jews for blowing up the World Trade Centers: "They got their people out." He has accused the Jews of "killing Christ" and said that "God condemns you." He has said that Jews set up the death of Martin Luther King Jr. He blames "the Jewish rabbis" and "the Talmud" for "the African holocaust." He has said that "the European Jews have America under control, lock, stock, and barrel, the media, foreign policy." He introduced a fellow anti-Semite named Khalid Abdul Muhammad, a man "who makes the Jews pee in their pants." He has railed against "the white, Jewish, Zionist onslaught" and has demanded that "all Jewish people and all white people... stop pushing your Holocaust down my throat." He led a Hitler-like question and answer chant at Howard University in which he asked the

Zionists must be "shut down" and have "no right to open [their] mouth anywhere on the planet."

No decent person should have anything to do with this anti-Semitic hatemonger, and every legitimate organization concerned about police abuse should disassociate itself from him and from his organization. Yet Cornel West, an intellectual leader of the intersectional movement, introduced this bigot at a "March of the Oppressed" rally outside the Republican National Convention in Cleveland, praising him as "my dear brother" whom he has known for twenty years and who "is still on the battlefield." He compared this rabid anti-Semite to the great Martin Luther King Jr. He asked the crowd to applaud for Shabazz, which they did. He then hugged him.[9] West's endorsement of Shabazz is comparable to a white professor introducing the grand wizard of the Ku Klux Klan with such effusive praise. Yet despite West's close association with and support for this advocate of genocide against Jewish babies, West was appointed to the Democratic Party platform committee by Bernie Sanders.

In short, intersectionality has succeeded in requiring its hard-left adherents to include anti-Zionism, anti-Americanism, and sometimes even violent rhetoric in the package of hard-left causes. It has also resulted in a systematic effort by many on the hard left to silence opponents of their radical politics. These radical censors argue that pro-Israel speech is hate speech that should be shut down, censured, and delegitimized. Students and faculty

---

assembled crowd, "Who committed crimes against the black people? Who controls the Federal Reserve?" After each question, he elicited the response: "Jews! Jews!" These quotations and others can be found at "Malik Zulu Shabazz: In His Own Words," adl.org, available at http://archive.adl.org/learn/ext_us/malik_zulu_shabazz/words.html.

who try to speak out against this left-wing bigotry are denied the "safe spaces," "trigger warnings," and protection from microaggression that the intersectionalists demand for themselves.

When I spoke at Johns Hopkins University in the fall of 2015, radical students claimed that I was "harassing" them by "remaining silent" and not admitting that Israel engaged in "genocide." Harassment by silence was a new one even for me!

The truth must be told about this intersectionality. Their practitioners are often not the progressive "good guys" whom I looked up to in my youth; they are repressive bullies and bigots who disguise their anti-Jewish, anti-Israel, anti-Christian, and anti-American bigotry as a quest for social justice. They must be fought—on campuses, at Democratic Party caucuses and conventions, and in the media—with the same righteous indignation with which decent people fight extreme right-wing manifestations of bigotry. Centrist leftists have a special obligation to criticize fellow leftists and Democratic extremist bigots, just as centrist Republicans have a special obligation to criticize bigotry on the extreme right such as that of Patrick Buchanan. That is why I, as a centrist liberal, devote so much time and energy to exposing the faults of the hard-left wing of the Democratic Party.

It is imperative that such radical identity politics and intersectional thinking does not spill over to the mainstream of the Democratic Party. The majority of Democrats are centrist and independent voters who do not think in these absurd packages of the hard left. Allowing such ideology to infiltrate our two-party system would not only be harmful for the Democrats but for the American political system as a whole. But the influence of the bigots within the Democratic Party is growing, as evidenced by the close votes and floor reactions regarding some of their agenda items.

This conflict between liberal and hard-left values, especially on campuses (where everything is exaggerated) augurs poorly for the future of traditional liberalism and of its place in the Democratic Party, and suggests that the conflict about which I am writing will only get worse as the students of today become the leaders of tomorrow. I still hope that traditional liberal values will win out in the end, much like they did a generation earlier when the radicalism embodied by Students for a Democratic Society, the Black Panthers, and the Weathermen gave way to the centrism of the Bill Clinton Democrats. But as the hard left's influence grows in the Democratic Party again, I worry that the party may be leaving me, and other centrist liberals, for good. They take our support for granted, because they think we have nowhere to go. We cannot vote for a Republican Party dominated by right-wing extremists who reject basic liberal values. Some traditional liberals could vote for a centrist Republican Party if there were one that reflected the influence of social moderates who favor liberty over religious compulsion, but that party is currently a memory, not a reality.

It is a tragedy that there is no longer a centrist Republican alternative to the Democratic Party. If there were, it would put pressure on Democrats to cultivate centrist voters instead of pandering to the hard left on many issues, both of foreign and domestic policy. But the Democratic Party leadership realizes that with the current Republican Party having been taken over by the hard religious right and the populist Donald Trump, centrist Democrats have little choice but to remain Democrats and vote for Democratic candidates, even if they disapprove of the growing influence of the hard left within the Democratic Party. They cannot vote for a party or candidate that opposes a woman's right to choose abortion, a gay man or woman's right to marry whomever they choose, a child's right to be safe from automatic weapons in the hands of psychopaths who were not required to undergo simple background checks, and other basic rights that have long been part of the liberal agenda. Nor can they vote for a candidate who has pledged to pack the Supreme Court with as many Justice Scalias as there are vacancies.

Both centrist Republicans and centrist Democrats benefit when *both* parties move away from extremes and toward the center, because centrism within one party begets centrism in the other, just as extremism in one party begets extremism in the other.

The Canary in the Coal Mine: Israel

There are three reasons I have focused on the anti-Israel aspect of the hard-left agenda that threatens the traditional centrism of the Democratic Party. First, it is the issue on which I receive the most emails, letters, and phone calls from erstwhile Democrats telling me that they can no longer vote for a party or for candidates that have moved away from supporting Israel and demanding to know how I can continue to support a party that is being hijacked by hard leftists who are committed to the Palestinian cause to the exclusion of other human rights issues. Second, I care deeply about Israel and share the concerns of those who have stopped voting for Democrats, though I myself continue to vote for most Democratic candidates in an effort to maintain bipartisan support for the nation-state of the Jewish people. And third, as is often the case, Israel may well be the canary in the coal mine—an early manifestation of a more general effort by the hard left to increase its influence within the Democratic Party in an effort to turn it from its centrist liberal roots toward a radical anti-liberal party. The American Democratic Party, unlike many European parties of the hard left, has not been overtly anti-Israel—at least not yet.

In most European countries, centrist conservative parties have generally been supportive of Israel, even if critical of some of its policies. Left-wing parties have a more mixed record. Leaders of center-left parties like France's François Hollande and Italy's Matteo Renzi, for example, have repeatedly defended Israel in the international arena. Far-left parties, however, have often taken the opposite approach.

In Norway, the Socialist Left Party has supported the BDS movement; in Spain, the populist left-wing party Podemos frequently posts and tweets anti-Semitic dog whistles and worse in its campaigns. One of its leaders tweeted in 2012 that Israel is "genocidal posing as an advanced democracy" and that it resembled Assad's regime in Syria. (These anti-Semitic rants did not stop Bernie Sanders from inviting a Podemos leader as his guest of honor to the DNC.) And in Italy, leaders of the populist Five Star Movement, which is now polling over the governing centrist Democratic Party, have accused Israel of genocide and run their successful campaigns on anti-Semitic canards reminiscent of the days of blood libels.

In the US, on the other hand, support for Israel has been largely bipartisan and our national policies relatively consistent. The Sanders campaign—and especially some of his most vocal supporters—challenged this bipartisan support and sought to reset the relationship in favor of a more anti-Israel, pro-Palestinian tilt. But that was merely one among many issues they pushed to influence the Democratic Party to move away from the centrist consensus that has long dominated American politics.

Polls show that Republican support of Israel is increasing as Democratic support, especially among young voters, diminishes. This is not about *particular* Israeli policies: I, too, disagree with the current Israeli approach to settlements on the West Bank. It is not what Israel *does*; it is about what Israel *is*: the nation-state of the Jewish people. The radical hard-left wing of the party—many of whose voters supported Bernie Sanders in the primaries and caucuses—have turned away from Israel, demonizing it as an apartheid, colonialist, and even genocidal state.

Radical organizations such as MoveOn, Occupy Wall Street, National Lawyers Guild, Code Pink, and Black Lives Matter have become overtly anti-Israel. Support for Israel among young Democrats on university campuses has diminished, as support for Israel among young and older Republicans has increased.

Although nearly all elected Democratic political leaders currently reject overt anti-Israel programs, such as the BDS movement, many Democratic voters, especially younger ones, support such programs. During the 2012 Democratic convention, delegates erupted in boos when their party declared Jerusalem to be Israel's capital.

During the 2016 presidential primary season, Bernie Sanders—who essentially ran on domestic issues—appointed overtly anti-Israel radicals to the platform committee in an effort to bring "balance" to the traditional bipartisan support for Israel.* He did this in an effort to satisfy the radical fringe of his supporters, for whom support for Israel is incompatible with progressive ideas. And at the 2016 Democratic convention, organizers arranged for pro-Clinton delegates to drown out the boos of Sanders's supporters by chanting, "Hillary, Hillary," when she expressed views they disagreed with, including support for Israel in the acceptance speech.[10]

Today, support for Israel comes largely from older liberals, from young traditional Jews, and from conservatives, including many evangelical Christians. Republican voters are more likely than Democratic voters to see Israel in a positive light.** Yet my generation of liberal Jews, and even the generations that followed mine, could not support a party or candidates that reject so many of our deeply felt

---

* One of the appointees, James Zogby, has described Gaza as "the world's largest concentration camp" and has repeatedly accused the Israeli government of perpetrating crimes against humanity. The other, the public intellectual Cornel West, has suggested that the Iraq War was caused by "the close relationship between American imperial elites and Israeli political officials." West has also repeatedly accused Israel of killing Palestinian babies—an allegation that echoes historic attacks on Jews for blood libel—and frequently claims that Israel is deliberately seeking to annihilate the Palestinian people.

** According to Pew, "There continue to be stark partisan differences in Middle East sympathies. Conservative Republicans maintain strong support for Israel with fully 75 percent saying they sympathize with Israel compared with just 2 percent who sympathize with the Palestinians. By contrast, liberal Democrats are much more divided: 33 percent sympathize more with Israel, 22 percent with the Palestinians."

liberal values. We continue to support Israel, though many of us disagree with some of its policies, especially with regard to civilian settlements in the West Bank. Unlike Bernie Sanders, our disagreements about specific policies do not generally carry over to Israel's security needs and its right to defend its citizens against rocket attacks, terrorism, and threats from Hezbollah, Hamas, and Iran. We do not believe, as Sanders does, that Israel's self-defense actions have been disproportionate, and we do believe that if any military actions are unlawful the Israeli judicial system is capable of dealing with them. We remain proudly pro-Israel and proudly liberal. But our numbers and influence within the left are shrinking. Liberal Zionists are an endangered species. And it will probably get worse, since younger liberals are less likely to support Israel than older ones.

On the Republican side, there have been concerns that Donald Trump has not acted decisively or quickly enough to condemn those of his hard-right supporters, such as David Duke, who are both anti-Jewish and anti-Israel. Few, if any, believe that Trump himself is anti-Semitic or anti-Zionist but, like Sanders, he seems unwilling to disassociate himself from his bigoted supporters. Many of Trump's hard-right pro-Israel supporters seem willing to excuse their candidate's softness on the anti-Semitism of some of his supporters because of their strong dislike for the Democratic Party and its candidate.

For supporters of Israel who are conservative on domestic issues and are willing to give Trump a pass on his many imperfections, there is little conflict: they simply vote Republican, without having to compromise their principles or ideologies. For Democrats who don't support

Israel but are liberal on domestic issues, there is also no conflict: simply vote Democrat. But for liberal supporters of Israel who, like me, cannot support Republican domestic programs, there *is* a conflict; we support most of the Democratic domestic agenda, but not necessarily its foreign policies, especially, but not exclusively, with regard to Israel.

The issue was put to me sharply for the first time in the 2012 presidential election. I supported with enthusiasm President Obama's domestic policies and his likely Supreme Court appointments. But I was worried about his policies with regard to Israel, and especially Iran. I expressed my concern in a series of op-eds in the *Wall Street Journal* and other media.[11] President Obama was certainly aware of these concerns among a segment of his base, and so he invited me to the Oval Office, where he assured me of his strong support for Israel and his firm commitment to preventing Iran from obtaining nuclear weapons. I wanted to believe him, because I didn't want there to be any conflict between my domestic liberal values and my deep concern about Israel's security. So I credited what he told me and campaigned and voted for his reelection, despite some lingering reservations.

The result of Obama's election and reelection was a positive domestic program—health care, gay marriage, liberal judicial appointments—coupled with deeply disappointing policies regarding Israel, especially Iran. Jewish conservatives, who voted against Obama and who don't like or don't care about his domestic policies, said, "See, I told you so." Jewish hard-left opponents of Israel, who were pleased with Obama with regard to both domestic and Israel policies, also said, "See, I told you so."

But many liberal supporters of Israel, like me, were conflicted. We will continue to be conflicted as long as Democrats who support liberal domestic principles are less supportive of Israel than Republicans who support Israel but are less supportive of liberal domestic policies.

Foreign Policy Beyond Israel

This conflict transcends Israel. There are many voters who strongly support the Democratic Party's domestic agenda but are deeply suspicious about its foreign policy in general. The Obama administration created a vacuum by abandoning America's role as the leader of the free world and as an active supporter of democracies. While many of us were opposed to the American occupation of Iraq, we favor a more muscular foreign policy and a robust role for America in maintaining liberal values around the world and in protecting the vital interests of America and its allies. We are not hawks nor are we doves.[12] We are realists who understand that the projection of American power is essential to maintaining peace and promoting liberal values. President Obama may have been awarded the Nobel Peace Prize shortly after taking office, but in the view of many liberals, the world became a more dangerous and less free place during his tenure. For many of us, the answer to Ronald Reagan's 1980 rhetorical question "Are you better off today than you were four years ago?" would depend on whether we are talking about domestic or foreign issues: we are better off at home, but there are reasonable doubts about whether we are better off or safer in the world at large.

Many of us were opposed to the Iran deal, but we do not favor a military attack on Iran, except perhaps as an absolute last resort to prevent that regime from acquiring a nuclear arsenal. We do not sing, "Bomb, bomb Iran," as Senator John McCain did during his presidential campaign. We want to keep a strong military option on the table, but without actually deploying the sword of Damocles unless absolutely necessary.[13]

The General Drift

Beyond the specifics of identity politics, intersectionality, and Israel, there is a more general concern among many centrist liberal Democrats about the party's drift toward hard-left radicalism. The same can be said for many centrist conservative Republicans, who are deeply concerned about the center of gravity of Abraham Lincoln's Grand Old Party.

The drift away from the center is palpable in both parties, from the applause lines that garner the loudest reactions, from the pandering to both extremes, and from other intangibles. And the signs all point to an increase, rather than a decrease, in the influence of extremes on both side of the political spectrum.

Those of us who have long been centrist liberals haven't left the left, nor have centrist Republicans left the right. The left, especially the radical left, has left us by abandoning traditional liberal values for radical extremism, just as the religious right has left the centrist right by abandoning the principles of Lincoln, Eisenhower, and even Reagan. What Ronald Reagan said in 1962 can be said of both parties today: "I didn't leave the Democratic Party; the Democratic Party left me."

The difference is that I and those who agree with me refuse to leave the Democratic Party. We want to fight *within* the party to restore its liberal center. Some centrist conservative friends feel the same way about the Republican Party. Some left-wing Democrats are moving away from the traditional Democratic approach to foreign policy, and many right-wing Republicans have moved toward an approach to social issues that is based more on fundamentalist religious values than on libertarian or traditional conservative values. We are seeking a third way, but in the end, because we are a nation with a two-party system, we will probably have to choose between the two existing, imperfect alternatives, while seeking to pressure both parties to move closer to our centrist values.

2

The Virtues and Vices of Unchecked Populism

The 2016 primary season saw the rise of populism, with the surprising victory of Donald Trump, a businessman with no political experience who became famous as the host of a popular TV show. It was not even clear before he decided to run whether he was a Democrat or Republican. After securing the Republican nomination with overwhelming popular victories in nearly every primary, he selected as his running mate Mike Pence, who began his career as a conservative radio talk show host before being elected to Congress and then the governorship of Indiana.

On the Democratic side, the strong showing by a relatively unknown senator from Vermont, Bernie Sanders, surprised everyone. His populist message—bring down Wall Street, end trade agreements that reduce American wages, increase taxes on the wealthy, provide a free college education at all public schools—smacked of class warfare, but it found receptive audiences among many young people, hard-left radicals, and angry and resentful white men and women. Although he ultimately lost the nomination, he succeeded in moving the Democratic Party and its candidate, Hillary Clinton, to the left on several important issues: Clinton abandoned her support for the Trans-Pacific Partnership (TPP)—which she helped to negotiate as President Obama's secretary of state—and she adopted Sanders's positions on raising the minimum wage, opposing the Keystone XL pipeline, and making college more affordable.[1] To her credit, she did not change her position on Israel, despite pressure from some Sanders supporters who were delegates and members of the Democratic platform committee.

There are, of course, many important differences between the populist campaigns conducted by Trump and Sanders, as there are between the candidates themselves. But there are also striking similarities. Both Trump and Sanders are political outsiders who are as far away from their respective establishments as any candidate in recent history. Both pander to the extremes of their base: Trump to hard-right bigots who hate minorities, immigrants, Muslims, Jews, and the "establishment"; Sanders to hard-left revolutionaries who hate Wall Street, the rich, Israel, and, again, the "establishment." Both have proposed popular but utterly unrealistic ideas that make for good sound bites: Trump has promised to build a wall between Mexico and the United States and have Mexico pay for it; to deport millions of illegal residents; to ban Muslim immigrants; to punish women who have abortions and their doctors; to bring manufacturing jobs back from countries like China and Mexico. His campaign promise to "make American great *again*" panders to his base supporters—white, less well-educated men who fear their status is eroding in an increasingly diverse society. Sanders, on the other hand, has proposed an expansion of government unseen since the New Deal, including a single-payer health care system, a "youth jobs program" designed to create one million jobs for young Americans, a massive expansion of Social Security, and a "college for all" program that would result in public colleges becoming tuition-free, regardless of the wealth of the student's family.[2] Although these are commendable goals, they are politically and fiscally unachievable. Various studies have estimated that Sanders's proposals would add at least $18 trillion to the deficit in the next decade,[3] while Trump's tax plan would result in a $10 trillion budget shortfall.[4]

Neither of these populist candidates has real experience in the rough and tumble of legislative negotiation and compromise. Trump has never held elective office, and Sanders, despite being in Congress for over thirty years, has always been an outsider and has had little success in getting important bills enacted—in his nine years in the Senate, Sanders cosponsored only one bill that passed in that chamber.[5] It is not surprising, therefore, that both of these populist candidates have run on a no-compromise platform: their way or the highway. No half loaves for them. Revolution, not evolution.

Both claim that their candidacies transcend any particular election. Both claim to have ignited a movement, regardless of whether they ultimately succeed or fail in getting elected. Both have passionate followers and equally passionate detractors.

The biggest difference, of course, is that Trump won his party's nomination, despite nearly unanimous opposition from the Republican Party establishment. Sanders lost to the candidate who had the near unanimous support of her party establishment. Some pundits have opined that right-wingers and the Republican Party are more vulnerable to populist appeals and candidates than are left-wingers or Democrats.[6] But the difference in outcome between the Democratic and Republican nominating processes is, perhaps, explainable by structural factors that currently distinguish the two parties. Trump ran against a field of sixteen nonincumbents and no single favorite who had the support of the Republican establishment, and it is far easier for a populist to win in a crowded field than in a head-to-head race with an establishment candidate. Senator Ted Cruz recognized this reality when he sought, but never managed to secure, a head-to-head contest between him and Trump.

Sanders ran not only in an uncrowded field—never more than four—but also against the presumptive nominee, who was as close to an incumbent as any nonpresident can be: a former first lady, senator, and secretary of state, and a party favorite who had many superdelegates wrapped up before a single vote was cast.

Had the shoe been on the other foot—had Trump been running against a single establishment "incumbent," and had Sanders been running against a crowded field—the results might have been different, though no one can know for sure. The general election in November 2016 will be a good head-to-head test of the power of populism, outsiderness, unpredictability, and instability versus the power of experience, insiderness, predictability, and stability.

The Sanders and Trump candidacies raise the question of whether populism is good or bad for governance. The answer is clearly yes. It has both good and bad qualities, as any objective review of history will demonstrate. When citizens vote for populist leaders, or for populist propositions in a referendum, they are, of course, exercising their most basic democratic right. The referendum, the town hall meeting, the direct election of national leaders—these are the purest manifestations of democracy. Perhaps that is why they are so rare. Few, if any, democracies today elect their national leaders directly. In the United States, we have the Electoral College, and there have been elections—Bush vs. Gore being the most recent—where the candidate with the most popular votes did not prevail. In Great Britain and most European democracies, national leaders are selected by the parliament, as seen most recently by the selection of Theresa May to become prime minister of the UK without any national election. And there has been much criticism of the decision by David Cameron to have put Brexit to a simple majority referendum, rather than to a parliamentary debate and vote.

Direct democracy, as distinguished from a system of checks and balances—including checks on the majority of voters in any given election—is controversial both in theory and practice, as evidenced by its complicated history in the United States.

Checking and Balancing Democracy

The Founding Fathers of our nation were as fearful of direct democracy as they were wary of tyranny. In fact, Alexander Hamilton and James Madison dedicated one of the most celebrated political essays of all time, Federalist Number 10, to denouncing the dangers of "pure democracy"—often referred to as "mobocracy"—which they felt was "incompatible with personal security or the rights of property."[7] They constructed, instead, a government of checks and balances, with three relatively coequal branches designed to serve as counterweights to each other.

Equally important, though less enduring, were the checks they imposed on the electorate itself. These included the indirect election of the president by the Electoral College, which was supposed to be composed of wise men, who would exercise judgment in the selection of the chief executive.

James Madison, the father of the Constitution, saw landholders as a "balance and check"[8] against the inevitable future voting power of the more numerous day laborers. He viewed the indirect election of senators as a protection of the "minority of the opulent against the majority."[9] The most significant compromise with democracy was, of course, the total disenfranchisement of the vast majority of the population: most states imposed voting restrictions on women, African-Americans, and those who did not own property. Remarkably, in the first presidential election in which the popular vote was tallied, the 1824 contest between John Quincy Adams and Andrew Jackson, the population of the United States was nearly ten million of which only 365,928 people voted—less than 4% of the population.*

---

* Ironically, Jackson, our first populist president won the popular vote 151,291 to 113,122 in 1824, four years before he became president, but the electoral college was tied, and the House of Representatives gave the election to J.Q. Adams in what Jackson supporters called the "corrupt bargain."

Moreover, in some counties and states there were further limitations: only Christians were qualified by law to vote or hold office, and in practice only Protestants were elected to high office. Senators were not elected by popular vote until 1890, and many elected officials were effectively selected by party bosses.

These limitations gradually ended, first with the advent of Jacksonian democracy, then Reconstruction, and later women's suffrage, and finally civil rights. And although there still exist extralegal barriers to voting in many parts of the country, the United States today is a far more democratic enterprise than what the founders might have expected: in theory, today all citizens over the age of eighteen—except for felons—have the right to vote, and nearly half of them actually do vote in presidential elections, in which the Electoral College now casts automatic votes based on the popular will.

Several innovations since the founding era have increased the power of the people in governance. In addition to the direct election of senators, the elimination of discretion by electors, and the enfranchisement of minorities, women, and young people, we have also witnessed the introduction of referenda, plebiscites, and recalls, which empower voters to have more direct impact on governance. In many states, prosecutors and judges are now elected, rather than appointed, thus making the justice system more political—for better or worse. These manifestations of Jacksonian democracy—a rejection of elitism that began with the election of our first populist president in 1828—have significantly changed the nature of governance by increasing the direct power of the electorate and lessening the influence of the elite.

At the same time, judicial review of the actions of the elective branches has increased, serving as a check against unconstitutional populism: the courts helped curb McCarthyism in the 1950s and combat institutionalized racism in the 1960s, sexism in the 1970s, and homophobia in recent years.

Other changes—the increasing role of twenty-four-hour TV, social media, primaries, and polls—have also altered our political system in ways that make populism more of a factor in elections. On the other hand, cases like *Citizens United* have enhanced the power of wealthy elites in the political process. It is beyond the ambit of this book to explore these important issues in any significant depth, but it is clear that in the past decade, populism has experienced a remarkable resurgence both in the United States—with the growth of political movements like the Tea Party and Occupy Wall Street, as well as the candidacies of Trump and Sanders—but also in many European nations. In the 2016 presidential election—both the primary and caucus processes, as well as the general election campaign—populism has played a significant role, as it did in the Brexit vote in Great Britain during that same time period.

What is wrong with populism? Is it not the true manifestation of democracy—the direct voice of the people, unfiltered by cumbersome political processes and checks? The answer to these questions may depend on whether one focuses on logic or experience. What Oliver Wendell Holmes famously said about law—"The life of the law has not been logic. It has been experience"—can also be said about politics and governance. In logic, populism *is* democracy. In experience, it has often been something different. Bernard-Henri Lévy characterized the populist Brexit vote as

> A victory not of the people but of populism ... not of democracy but of demagogy. It is a victory of the hard right over the moderate right and of the radical over the liberal left. It is a victory of xenophobia in both camps ... of drunken skinheads and hooligans, of illiterate rebels and bullheaded neo-nationalists.[10]

This was perhaps an overstatement issued in anger and fear, but it reflects a widespread attitude toward the alleged evils of untrammeled populism run amok.

The consequences of populism tend to be extreme, because they are unfiltered by the checks and balances of processes and institutions that often require compromise to reach an acceptable result. The political differences between institutional democracy and direct popular democracy are in some respects analogous to the religious differences between Catholicism and Protestantism, or between rabbinic and Karaite Judaism. The Catholic Church and the rabbinic authorities serve as intermediaries between believers, their God, and their Scriptures. Catholics read and understand the Bible through the church. Orthodox Jews interpret the Torah through rabbinic *halacha*. Protestantism and Karaism, on the other hand, eliminate the intermediaries and encourage direct interaction with God and his Scriptures. It is expected that the Catholic Church and Jewish rabbis would have a stabilizing, moderating effect on religious extremism. This has sometimes, but not always, been the case.

The very concept of democracy is, and has always been,

a matter of degree. No country has ever operated under pure direct democracy, though single-body parliamentary systems come closer, at least in theory, than the American system of division of powers and checks and balances. Small towns, with their open town-hall meetings, come closest to direct democracies, but that model is not adaptive to governing large and complex governmental units. Indeed, over time, bureaucracy transcends democracy as the so-called administrative state makes many of the most significant day-to-day decisions that impact the lives of voters, without much direct input from, or accountability to, voters. (This was one of the complaints the pro-Brexit voters had against the bureaucrats who run the European Union from Brussels, without much input from their constituents in Great Britain and elsewhere.) Theory and practice are quite different when it comes to governance of large and complex democracies.

Even in the earliest days of the new republic, when Alexis de Tocqueville traveled through America, he had difficulty describing the nature of American democracy, especially with regard to where sovereignty resides, since there was no king or emperor and the American president was subject to legislative and judicial checks. In spirit, he concluded, it was in the bosoms of its people. But in practice, "the nation participates in the making of its laws by the choice of its legislators, and in the execution of them by the choices of the agents of the executive government."[11] Sovereignty in America was, and still is, a *process* of checks and balances, with different institutions increasing their power—and the need to be checked and balanced by other institutions—over time and place. At bottom, however, these competing institutions must never "forget their popular origin and the [ultimate] power from which they emanate"[12]—namely the people.

But history has shown that there is a difference between the people exercising their power directly through referenda, town meetings, and the election of populist—often authoritarian—candidates on the one hand, and on the other, indirectly through a process of democratic checks and balances. As the great human rights activist Natan Sharansky has said, "Democracy means both free democratic elections and a free democratic society."[13]

There are numerous examples throughout history and currently of popularly elected undemocratic dictators, and of dictators who would have been elected if they had permitted free and open elections. Hitler is an example of the latter: he had enormous popular support throughout Germany even after he suspended civil liberties, targeted dissenters, and imposed discriminatory laws against Germans of Jewish descent. Mao, Stalin, and Castro also had widespread popular support, as do Erdoğan, Putin, and Hungary's Viktor Orbán today.

Republican and Democratic Parties as Checks on Populism

Our system of checks and balances has come, over time, to include the two major political parties. Such was not always the case: the founding generation was wary of political parties. But over the years, the Republican and Democratic establishments have developed a "crucial role as intermediating institution[s] in US politics—namely, providing responsible political opposition and governing alternatives and vetting candidates to weed out crackpots, demagogues, and mountebanks who have no business holding public office."[14] This election cycle has seen the Democratic establishment succeed in nominating a centrist candidate, while the Republican Party nominated a fringe populist. There are several structural factors underlying this phenomenon, but the most important among them may have been the success of the Democratic establishment over the past decade to deliver concrete if imperfect results to its constituents—health care reform, the legalization of gay marriage, and stronger environmental regulations, to name a few—and the concurrent failure of its Republican counterpart to deliver for its base.

As a result—and despite the fierce criticisms directed against the DNC by the hard left—Democratic voters have shown more trust in their so-called party elders, followed President Obama's lead, and backed the establishment candidacy of Hillary Clinton. The Republican Party, on the other hand, has spent the past eight years vilifying President Obama in increasingly conspiratorial terms—they have called him a communist, they have suggested that he was born in Kenya, they have described Obamacare as a precursor to fascism[15]—and yet for all the vitriol, they have failed to defeat Obama electorally or roll back his policy achievements. For nearly a decade now, Republican politicians of all stripes have accused President Obama and his liberal agenda of diminishing America; perhaps it should come as no surprise that their electorate has nominated someone whose motto is "Make America Great Again" and who openly embraces fringe conspiracy theories peddled by extremists within the conservative punditry.

Other more-technical factors are important as well; in particular, the Republican Party, unlike the Democratic Party, has no superdelegates, whose job it is to serve as a check on the popular votes and think about the long-term interests of the party and the nation. In this respect the Republican Party is, ironically, more democratic than the Democratic Party, with its elitist superdelegates, some of whom do not even hold elective office.

Another reason may be the unwillingness or inability of the Republican Party to narrow the field of candidates to a handful or less, so that one of them would emerge with a clear majority of the total votes cast. The Republican debates, with a large number of candidates, made it impossible for candidates to express complex and nuanced policy positions. The formats and the numbers of speakers gave a palpable advantage to a populist candidate like Trump, whose simplistic bumper-sticker points, personal attacks, demagoguery, and charisma could stand out from the crowded field. Trump managed to turn the primary campaign into a one-on-fifteen confrontation: him against the rest of the field. By the time the field narrowed, Trump had all but wrapped up the nomination.

The opposite was true of the Democratic primary process, which quickly narrowed to a head-to-head competition between the populist candidate Sanders and the establishment candidate Clinton, with her superdelegates in the bag. Sanders railed against what he called the undemocratic process of nominating a candidate for president. Although by all reasonable democratic criteria—total number of popular votes, delegates won in primaries, total number of non-superdelegates—Clinton secured a clear victory, it is true that both in theory and practice, the

Democratic Party process is more skewed in favor of establishment candidates and against populist outsiders than the Republican Party. A Republican populist outsider has a better chance of securing his party's presidential nomination than does a Democratic populist outsider. It may also be true, though there is no evidence to support it, that regardless of the structural differences, Republican voters, especially current Republican voters, are more susceptible to the lure of populist candidates than Democratic voters.

The end result of these differences between the parties will be a general election pitting a populist Republican against an establishment Democrat; an unpredictable candidate with no governmental experience against an entirely predictable candidate with a long record of diverse experiences as a first lady (both to a governor and a president), a senator, and a secretary of state; and a destabilizing candidate who shoots from the hip and engages in personal vendettas against a force for stability, who carefully measures her words and bases her actions (at least most of the time) on tested policies.

There are, of course, other factors that distinguish the candidates: Trump sees the world in categories—*the* blacks, *the* Mexicans, *the* women, *the* gays, *the* Jews; Clinton too focuses on group rights of women, gays, minorities, working people, but she tends not to stereotype as much as Trump. Trump panders to the religious right, despite his own spotty record as a Christian (three marriages, claims of affairs with married women,[16] using scatological language against his opponents). Clinton has been accused of sometimes pandering to the hard left, co-opting Sanders's "progressive" label, but adding "who gets things done." As discussed in subsequent chapters, Trump supports much of the Republican conservative platform opposing abortion, gay marriage, gun control, financial regulation, and other issues. Clinton supports the Democratic platform supporting all of the above and other liberal policies.

But at the bottom, Trump is not running as a policy candidate. His supporters are voting for him because of who he *is*, not because of the policies he espouses. Indeed, many of his voters have no idea where he actually stands on abortion, gay rights, and other divisive social issues, because he has been all over the place on these issues over time. They want *him* to be president because they like his independence, his willingness to say what he thinks, his "America-first" attitude, and his in-your-face style. They believe he is their "voice" and he "alone" can "make American great again." In a word, they like his populism.

It may seem strange that the most successful populist candidate in modern history is a New York City multi-millionaire who started his career as a landlord and who made his fortune on upscale real estate; has become famous for firing people; has exploited bankruptcy laws to hurt small-business owners, workers, and other creditors; has insulted large groups of people comprising a majority of voters (women, Latinos, the physically challenged, Muslims); has used vulgar words on TV that offend Christians, parents of young children, and family-oriented people of all backgrounds. He has disrespected veterans like John McCain, who was wounded in combat and held in enemy captivity for more than five years; and the Gold Star mother and father of Humayun Khan, a Muslim American who sacrificed his life in an effort to save fellow soldiers. But he may have turned some of these apparent weaknesses into strengths by insisting that "the Donald" is the only public figure in America who says what he thinks and isn't afraid of the consequences. As he boasted: "I could stand in the middle of Fifth Avenue and shoot somebody and I wouldn't lose voters." This is reminiscent of the boast made by Edwin Edwards, the populist former three-term governor of Louisiana: "The only way I can lose is if I'm caught in bed with either a dead girl or a live boy." When Edwards ran against another populist—David Duke, the former grand wizard of the Ku Klux Klan—he boasted of his sexual indiscretions: "The only thing we have in common is we're both wizards under the sheets." Bumper stickers in support of the allegedly corrupt governor read: "Vote for the crook. It's important," and "Vote for the crook, not the racist." He won a runoff election over the grand wizard. (Both eventually served time in prison for fraud.)*

The point is that a successful populist can often turn vices into virtues, as Trump has done. He has used the F word on TV, criticized John McCain for having been captured in combat operations during the Vietnam War, attacked the parents of a soldier killed in combat, suggested that a popular TV newsperson was menstruating when she asked him a tough question, bragged about his sexual infidelities and the size of his penis, mocked a physically challenged journalist, suggested that many immigrants from Mexico are rapists, and implied that Ted Cruz's father had a hand in the JFK assassination. And he has gained support in the process! That is a true test of a populist: to make his foibles seem human and to capitalize on them to secure popular support. Another true test of a populist is whether he can persuade voters that only *he* can solve problems of

---

* I helped represent Governor Edwards on one of his appeals. I liked him, personally. He was warm, charming, witty, and smart.

the day. Trump is seeking to do that, as evidenced by his acceptance speech, which was light on issues and heavy on selling himself to voters as their charismatic leader.

Can a Woman Be a Populist?

The success of populists like Trump and Edwards, among other male populists throughout our history, raises an interesting and important question: Can only a man be a successful populist candidate today—or could a woman, with attributes similar to Trump's, also succeed as a populist candidate?

It is difficult to come up with the names of many successful past or contemporary female populists: Sarah Palin (John McCain's running mate for vice president) and Marine Le Pen, leader of the Front National in France, come to mind. But neither of them has been elected to high office. Among the increasing number of successful women national leaders—Golda Meir, Margaret Thatcher, Angela Merkel, Theresa May—none can be considered populists. Each worked their way to the top of the establishment based on hard work, strong policies, and support from fellow party members. None were braggarts, demagogues, or peacocks. None boasted about their sexual exploits, corruption, or ability to get elected in spite of their misdeeds.

Populism may well be reserved for the male of the species, at least as long as we continue to operate under a double standard of expectation for successful men and women. Consider the Clintons. It is widely believed that Bill has engaged in sexual indiscretions. Yet it is Hillary who is blamed for her husband's misconduct: Why didn't she leave him? Why did she enable him? Why did she cover for him? How could she have allowed it? If Bill Clinton could run for a third term now, he would probably win overwhelmingly. *His* indiscretions would not be held against *him*. But they are being held against *her*!

No woman who said the things that Trump has said could ever be considered as a serious candidate. We simply expect more, or at least different, of women candidates than of men. We want "our" women leaders to be "ladies," but we don't expect the men to be gentlemen. Boys will be boys! Women must be beyond reproach. That is one reason why so much more attention is being paid to Hillary Clinton's email issue than to the many "extremely careless" things Donald Trump has done.*

Populism in a candidate is not gender neutral. It is for men only. Women need not apply. Among the most important differences between the two current candidates may well be that Trump is a man and Clinton is a woman.

---

* The statement by FBI director James Comey regarding Clinton's carelessness had an immediate negative impact on her poll numbers. I wrote critically of Comey's authority, or lack thereof, to make such a statement. (Alan Dershowitz, "Did FBI Director Comey Exceed his Authority?", *The Hill*, July 6, 2016). "It is not generally regarded as the job of the FBI to make calls about whether or not to prosecute. Those judgment calls are supposed to be made by prosecutors." (Alan Dershowitz, "Comey May Have Gone Too Far," *USA Today*, July 7, 2016.) Nor is it usual for an FBI director to express opinions such as that Clinton was "extremely careless" in her handling of sensitive material. Comey himself was "extremely careless" when he said that a small number of the emails "bore markings indicating the presence of classified material." This was widely but mistakenly understood to suggest that they were explicitly stamped "confidential." In my public statements, I asked him to clarify, and he did, explaining that some emails "bore the notation (C), indicating that it was classified as 'confidential,'" but none was expressly stamped confidential. (See "FBI Director James Comey Testifies Before Congress," *New York Times*, July 7, 2016.)

Each will gain and lose votes on account of their gender. That is obvious and fairly overt: some voters will vote for Clinton because they want to see a woman president, just as some voted for Obama because they wanted to see a black president. Some will vote against her because they don't want a woman president, just as some voted against Obama because they didn't want a black president. Gender and race matter in elections, as they do in other aspects of life. But more subtle, even unconscious, factors may be at play here as well: some voters will expect more from a female than from a male candidate.

That isn't fair, but it may be real. President Obama has said about Hillary Clinton that "there has never been a man or a woman, not me, not Bill, nobody more qualified than Hillary Clinton to serve as president of the United States of America."[17] Even for those who regard this as somewhat hyperbolic,* there can be little doubt that she is far more experienced, and by the usual standards far more qualified than the man she is running against, who has zero experience at any level of government. Yet the election appears at this writing to be a close one. Would it be as close if a man — say, Joe Biden — with experience and qualifications comparable to Hillary Clinton's were running against Donald Trump? We will never know for certain, but it is Hillary Clinton, a powerful and experienced woman, who is running against Donald Trump. This election will pit a woman against a man; an insider with considerable experience against an outsider with no governmental experience; an establishment candidate against a populist; a policy wonk against a relative unknown with no

* George H. W. Bush had been a congressman, ambassador to China, ambassador to the UN, director of the CIA, chair of the Republican National Committee, and vice president.

record of consistent policies; a liberal who is moving left-ward against a nonideologue who has moved rightward; a stabilizing force against an unpredictable hip-shooter. All of these differences are likely to influence voters in the 2016 election. That is what makes it so difficult to predict the outcome, and why it is imperative for every eligible voter who cares about the future of our country and the world to exercise their right to vote in this critical election, even if they're not aroused by either candidate.

It is better for democracy if a president is elected because a majority of the voters wanted to see that candidate in office than if a president is elected because a majority didn't want to see his or her opponent elected. Either Hillary Clinton or Donald Trump will become the president of the United States. Voting *against* a candidate who will be a bad president is as legitimate a basis for casting a ballot as voting *for* a candidate who will be a good president. But the worst thing for democracy is for a president to be elected because a great many citizens decided not to vote for either candidate.

European Populism: "Make Hungary Great!"

As we contemplate the possibility of a populist presidency here in the United States, it is useful to examine how this rebirth of political populism is impacting the European political landscape. Indeed, the experiences of Eastern Europe in particular may offer a cautionary tale for the American electorate. The populist right has already assumed power in several European countries and is experiencing a resurgence in traditional centrist strongholds like the United Kingdom, France, and Germany. The populist left has also experienced a rebirth within some traditionally centrist liberal political parties, such as Labour in Great Britain, and in some southern European countries like Greece, Italy, and Spain.

In some instances, the old labels of left and right are difficult to apply to this new form of politics because its proponents—like Trump—rarely subscribe to consistent political ideologies. In fact, they seem to reject the political institutions of a system they view as part corrupt and part impotent. They increasingly embrace policy positions that are inherently contradictory and premised on an emotional reaction to current socioeconomic circumstance. In short, populism has returned to many parts of the old continent. While in most well-established Western democracies the centrist consensus continues to hold, since 2010 several Eastern European countries have experienced dramatic turns away from the traditional liberal political system promoted by the European Union. Increasingly, Eastern Europe is attempting to navigate the uncharted waters of illiberal, autocratic populism of a variety not seen since the 1930s.

Between the fall of the Berlin Wall in 1989 and the financial crisis of 2008, the European electorate broadly empowered centrist parties from both the right and the left.*

---

* Germany, for example, elected the center-right CDU (Christian Democratic Union) in 1982, then the center-left SPD (Social Democratic Party) in 1998, before again settling on the CDU in 2005. In Hungary, the center-left liberals first elected in 1994 were replaced by a center-right coalition in 1998, followed by a center-left coalition in 2002. France, for its part, saw the center-left socialist party of François Mitterrand replaced by the center-right coalition of Jacques Chirac in 1996, followed by another center-right government led by Nicolas Sarkozy in 2006.

To varying degrees, these parties pursued centrist liberal policy goals, in line with the founding principles of the European Union. While left and right differed on how to strike the correct balance between, for example, strengthening the social security net and encouraging economic growth, they generally promoted an agenda that advanced the rule of law through an independent judiciary, respect for basic human rights, and freedom of the press. Above all, they pushed for a more integrated Europe both economically and politically.

The financial crisis of 2008 unraveled this political consensus and discredited the ruling center-left and center-right parties, particularly in Eastern Europe, which was never entirely comfortable with the sudden turn to centrist liberalism that followed the collapse of the Soviet Union. In several former Soviet bloc countries, the populist right has profited from the demise of the liberal center. The grey and sometimes corrupt bureaucrats who governed those countries in the 1990s and early 2000s have been replaced by irreverent, bombastic, and autocratic strongmen who promised to restore national pride and rebuild the economy through political upheaval on a grand scale.

Hungary offers an interesting case study in this regard.* In 2010, Hungarians overwhelmingly elected Viktor

---

* Between 1994 and 2010, various center-left– and center-right–led governments helped implement a program of economic and political liberalization that culminated in Hungary joining the EU in 2004. In 2008, however, following the collapse of the Hungarian currency, the forint, support for the ruling center-left coalition eroded almost overnight. In 2009, the far-right party Jobbik—one of whose candidates promised to end the "degenerate, sick liberal hegemony" and to "declare war on the sick liberal entertainment state"—won nearly 15 percent of the vote in elections for the European Parliament, and the following year, Viktor Orbán came to power.

Orbán and his nominally center-right Fidesz party. Orbán had once espoused a quasi-libertarian political platform, but recognizing the prevailing political climate, he campaigned on a promise to rewrite the constitution and to "Make Hungary Great"[18] by taking powers from the European Union and giving them back to the federal government. (In a predictable twist, Orbán recently endorsed Donald Trump for president.)[19]

Upon assuming power, Orbán embarked on a crusade to rid Hungary of "unpatriotic" elements that undermined the authority of the government. In particular, he passed a series of laws limiting freedom of the press.* This was followed by constitutional reforms in 2011 that effectively abolished the independence of the judiciary and solidified the power of Orbán's party by restructuring the electoral districting system.

Since then, Orbán's government has leaned farther and farther to the right. Indeed, several members of Orbán's government and many of its supporters have veered steadily into the realm of outright anti-Semitism. In 2014, Orbán himself redesignated a memorial to the Holocaust in Budapest as a memorial to all Hungarians killed during the German occupation,[20] sparking widespread international condemnation. In response, one of Orbán's deputies launched a tirade against the "cosmopolitan, internationalist left-liberal elite"—an obvious code phrase for the Jews—who "would still like to prescribe whom we can mourn and whom we can't, for whom we can shed a tear and for whom we can't."[21]

---

* In particular, Orbán created a regulatory body with the power to sanction media outlets for "content violations," and in some cases to suspend publishing licenses altogether. A new law also required media organizations to promote "national identity" in their reporting.

In May 2016, I personally experienced what I have characterized as the end of the seventy-year "moratorium on Jew-hatred" in Europe that followed the Holocaust. During my visits to Poland, Hungary, Slovakia, and Austria, I saw that Jews in parts of Europe are once again "caught between the extremes of the black and the red"—the classic anti-Semitism of the hard right and now anti-Zionism and sometimes anti-Semitism of the hard left.[22]

Orbán's Hungary is an extreme but hardly an isolated example of populism gone haywire in Eastern Europe. Since the 2008 financial meltdown, and more recently in the wake of the migrant crisis, Slovakia, Poland, and the Czech Republic have all embraced nationalistic and strikingly anti-liberal agendas.* Turkey—one of the few functional Islamic democracies in the Middle East—has also empowered its own strongman, Recep Tayyip Erdoğan, who seems intent on implementing his own distinct form of populist autocracy, particularly following the attempted military coup this summer.

Even the more established democracies of Western Europe have not been immune to the rising tide of populism. Since taking the leadership of the French Front

---

* Slovakia's prime minister, Robert Fico, for example, has curtailed freedom of the press while simultaneously stoking anti-Roma, anti-Muslim, and anti-Hungarian sentiment. The Czech Republic has veered from Thatcherite conservatism to a unique blend of populism premised primarily on anti-EU, anti-liberal resentment. Poland has seen the most marked transformation. Until recently, it was the model child of EU-style liberalism: since its accession to the free-labor zone in 2004, it experienced rapid economic growth and a marked increase in living standards. But since the election of the far-right populist Law and Justice Party in 2016, it has taken notable steps to walk back the liberal status quo: in particular it has severely limited the autonomy of the free press and repeatedly censored journalists and other writers critical of government policies or Polish pride.

National in 2011, Marine Le Pen has injected new life into French far-right politics, by combining racist dog whistles with a powerful economic populism that explicitly condemns EU-style liberalism.* Her formula has found similarly fertile ground in Germany, where the far-right Alternative für Deutschland (AFD) party has made recent inroads at a municipal level. With its anti-immigrant stance, the AFD's influence is likely to grow. As the *New York Times* reported after four closely spaced acts of terrorism in Germany in July: "Since the attacks, leaders from the centrist parties have been offering detailed suggestions for policy changes to counter terrorism, a desperate attempt to the prove the ability of mainstream politics to respond. But however sensible their suggestions, none of them can compete with easy populist slogans like 'No asylum for Muslims' or 'Shut the borders.'"[23] Far-left populist parties have also experienced a resurgence across Western Europe, including in France and Germany—where the far-left Die Linke is now the third-largest party in parliament. This is most notable in Spain, where the anti-EU, anti-liberal Podemos party—the party whose leader was invited by Sanders to be his guest at the Democratic National Convention[24]—is now the second-largest political coalition.

Despite their nominal characterization as left or right, the new FN in France, the AFD and Die Linke in Germany, and Podemos in Spain each embrace positions from both sides of the political spectrum. Both the FN and the AFD, for example, are staunchly pro-environment and opposed

* Le Pen is projected to win the second largest number of votes in France's 2017 presidential election, and her party has already scored major victories in regional elections.

to big business and free trade—both positions that are traditionally associated with the left of the political spectrum, and embraced by Podemos. The Five Star Movement in Italy epitomizes the ideological ambiguity that defines the new European populism: Beppe Grillo—the party leader, whose major CV item is as a stand-up comedian—is at once anti-immigrant (and borderline racist), anti-militarist, anti-globalist, and anti-Israel.*

These amorphous policy platforms, coupled with anti-establishment movement politics, should seem eerily familiar to any observer of the current American political scene: whether by intent or happenstance, Trump (and to a lesser extent Sanders) is following the playbook of Grillo, Le Pen, and their more successful Eastern European counterparts. Like them, he is channeling the widespread discontent felt by a large swath of the electorate with the existing socioeconomic system and the centrist establishment. This is not to suggest that Trump would be capable of achieving the kind of impact Orbán has in Hungary, because the political, judicial, and media establishments are far more entrenched in the United States than they were in the former Soviet bloc countries—but it is worth noting that very few political commentators expected Orbán (and Slovakia's Fico) to be able to cement power so effectively,

---

* Grillo's major policy items are pushing for electronic elections and promoting referenda as a tool of government. And while Grillo's populism has yet to draw in a majority of the electorate—indeed, much like Le Pen in France, and the AFD in Germany, most commentators remain convinced that he has a relatively low ceiling of support—he is impacting the political process in meaningful ways. Rome recently elected a mayor from the Five Star Movement who promises to enact significant elements of Grillo's agenda on a local level. The one defining quality of his leadership has been his emphasis on direct—or "zero cost"—democracy.

nor for Le Pen to emerge as one of the leading contenders for the French presidency in 2017.

The United Kingdom—the longtime bastion of centrist politics—offers further evidence of the dangers of underestimating this modern populism. In the past year, the moderate British political establishment has imploded in dramatic fashion. First, in the wake of a second successive electoral defeat, the Labour Party tacked hard to the left by electing as its leader Jeremy Corbyn, an old-school leftist revolutionary, who has quickly let anti-Semitism infect his party*; then the conservative Tory party saw itself blindsided by the Brexit campaign and the populist insurgency of Nigel Farage and Boris Johnson. In response, the more centrist elements of the Tory party have recently sought to co-opt this populist anger by bringing Johnson into the fold as the foreign minister in Prime Minister Theresa May's new cabinet. But regardless of these efforts, Brexit remains a historic slap in the face to the centrism promoted by the British political class. Following the British vote to leave the European Union, former prime minister Tony Blair bemoaned the loss of power by "the political center," of which he was a leader—and the growing influence of both "the far left and far right."[25]

He warned that instability will increase unless the center can "regain its political traction, rediscover its capacity

---

* Jeremy Corbyn, the Labour leader since 2015, embraces a type of revolutionary politics akin to those promoted by Bernie Sanders. Labour's turn left has been accompanied by some unfortunate side effects, in particular accusations that Corbyn's administration has been far too tolerant of anti-Semitic comments by his party members. Moreover, the new Labour party platform more closely resembles an old-school socialist screed—replete with promises to nationalize various industries—than the pragmatic center-left politics successfully promoted by Tony Blair.

to analyze the problems we all face and find solutions that rise above the populist anger."[26]

It could happen in the United States as well, if the center fails to hold. The Republicans have nominated a candidate who is about as far from the sensible and predictable center as any candidate in recent history. Republican primary and caucus voters rejected centrist candidates such as Jeb Bush, John Kasich, and Marco Rubio. Democratic voters cast millions of ballots for a populist candidate from the extreme left whose supporters included advocates of violence, revolution, and civil disobedience.

What is striking about the rise of populism in America is that, unlike its Eastern European counterparts, it seems to be triumphing at a time of relative prosperity and peace. Yet in this increasingly polarized political climate—with its twenty-four-hour news cycle and social media landscape—facts often yield to misguided fear and emotions, especially when these fears and emotions are exploited by populist demagogues.

At the RNC, Republicans seized on the theme of "law and order," even though the numbers of violent crimes in big cities have gone down to a record low. As the Nobel Prize–winning economist Paul Krugman observed in his *New York Times* column:

New York is now basically as safe as it has ever been, going all the way back to the nineteenth century. National crime statistics, and numbers for all violent crimes, paint an only slightly less cheerful picture. ... How, then, was it even possible for Donald Trump to give a speech accepting the Republican nomination whose central premise was that crime is running rampant, and that "I alone" can bring the chaos under control? ... Yet there's no question that many voters—including, almost surely, a majority of white men—will indeed buy into that vision. Why?[27]

When a CNN reporter at the RNC confronted former Speaker Newt Gingrich with the fact that the violence has dropped in major cities, he responded:

> The average American, I will bet you this morning, does not think crime is down, does not think they are safer. The current view is that liberals have a whole set of statistics which theoretically may be right, but it's not where human beings are. People are frightened. People feel that their government has abandoned them.

When the reporter pressed Gingrich, saying that "set of statistics" is not from liberal organizations but from the FBI, Gingrich, a former professor of history, said tellingly:

> What I said is equally true. People feel it. As a political candidate, I'll go with how people feel and I'll let you go with the theoreticians.[28]

To some extent, the elevation of feelings over facts is nothing new for Republicans. In previous elections, they have denounced climate change as a hoax, despite almost universal scientific agreement on the issue, and in this current election cycle, they declared that there is a war on Christianity, even though spirituality and religiosity have gone up in recent years. (The US is virtually the only Western democracy where that is the case.)

Why is it now acceptable to think that only because

one *feels* something is true that therefore this makes it true? Krugman offers the following hypothesis:

> Trump supporters really do feel, with some reason, that the social order they knew is coming apart. It's not just race, where the country has become both more diverse and less racist (even if it still has a long way to go). It's also about gender roles—when Trump talks about making America great again, you can be sure that many of his supporters are imagining a return to the (partly imagined) days of male breadwinners and stay-at-home wives.[29]

There is certainly some truth to that, but it is also true that many people fall prey to the so-called availability bias, which causes people to overestimate probabilities of an event associated with memorable, recent, or dramatic occurrences. For example, people overestimate the numbers of plane crashes because the images of a highly reported plane crash come more immediately to mind than the uncounted times of an unreported safe landing. Similarly, people are likely to overestimate the chances of a terrorist attack after having just learned about one elsewhere, or they are likely to overestimate the number of police abuses against blacks after having seen the powerful images of such an incident. In an age of social media—where people seek out information they agree with—the danger of such availability bias only grows.[30]

That does not mean that these fears are unfounded and that these problems should not be addressed. It just explains that individuals' feelings and perceptions are frequently not supported by the actual numbers. Terrorists know that, and their success thrives on this tactic. So do politicians.

Finally, there is the visible reality that the gap between the super-rich and the working class has widened. As the super-rich grow richer and richer and the working classes stagnate, the perception grows that workers are getting poorer and poorer, even for those whose economic situation has not grown worse in absolute terms.

Typically, challenging parties are better able to capitalize on emotions and fears that they themselves have helped to conjure. The incumbent party cannot do this, lest it diminish the party's legacy. When President Obama tried to push back after the recent police shootings in Dallas, by correctly pointing out that our racial tensions are not what they were in the 1960s, he was criticized for being insensitive and out of touch.

In short, while there is little agreement between the candidates and their parties about substantive issues, there is agreement about the unstable state of the world and about divisions within the country. Donald Trump has said repeatedly that "the world is falling apart," while Bill Clinton, speaking as his wife's surrogate, observed that "a lot of things are coming apart around the world right now."[31]

The remedies the candidates propose to deal with these instabilities, however, are almost diametrically opposed. Trump has pledged to emulate former president Nixon: "I think what Nixon understood is that when this world is falling apart, people want a strong leader whose highest priority is protecting America first."[32] Secretary Clinton, by contrast, has argued that the solutions to the challenges facing the country can be solved by "millions of Americans coming together": "if we stand together, we will rise together. Because we are stronger together."[33]

A world with wide pendulum swings between the hard right and the hard left is a dangerous place. We will be safer in a centrist world, but politicians are averse to campaigning from the middle. Centrism has become synonymous with a boring and dysfunctional political status quo, and there is great temptation—especially at a time of increasing popular unrest—to pander to the extremes embodied by the "movement" politics that define the Donald Trump and Bernie Sanders candidacies. But this temptation must be resisted in the name of much-needed stability. The stakes are now higher than the future of the United States. What is at stake in this election is the future stability of the world.

3

The Case Against Democracy by Default

Make a Checklist and Vote

In all my years of observing and participating in American politics, I have never seen a situation where so many citizens who have always voted in past elections have said, "I can't vote for either candidate in this election." Others have put it a bit differently: "How could American democracy present us with this choice?"

Although I am personally quite comfortable voting for one of the candidates, I understand why some Americans dislike the choice with which they have been presented. Some say they will vote for a third-party candidate, either the more centrist Johnson/Weld Libertarian ticket or the Stein/Baraka Green Party ticket. If a significant number of voters do vote for a third or fourth party, this could impact the election, as the votes for Ralph Nader in 2000 may have determined the Florida outcome, which in turn determined the general election outcome. It is unlikely that Stein will garner sufficient votes to have an impact; she is a bizarre outlier representing extreme positions far to the left of Bernie Sanders that have little to do with the environment.* Moreover, she selected as her vice presidential candidate Ajamu Baraka, a rabidly anti-Israel and anti-American radical who has accused Israel of war crimes, and described the United States as a "rogue state" that has consistently "demonstrated contempt for international law, human rights, and... the equal value of all human life."[1]

But it is possible that the more mainstream Johnson/ Weld ticket could draw votes more heavily from one party than the other in closely contested states. That too is part of democracy.

But under our two-party system, a vote for a third or fourth party is either a throwaway vote or a vote against one of the two major candidates. I believe it is incumbent upon Americans to vote and I also believe that every vote

* For example, Stein has expressed support for the idea that Quantitative Easing be applied to student debt; she has argued that the federal government should provide medical funding for the support of "alternative therapies" such as "homeopathy" and "naturopathy"; she has seemed sympathetic to anti-vaccine conspiracy theories, and she has described Julian Assange as "a hero." See Jordan Weissman, "Jill Stein's Ideas Are Terrible. She Is Not the Savior the Left is Looking For," *Slate*, July 27, 2016, and Eli Watkins, "Jill Stein: 'No Question' Julian Assange is a Hero," *CNN*, August 6, 2016. Despite Stein's attempts to consolidate a sizeable national following in the 2016 election, the Green Party remains dominated by a fringe of "people that could be—affectionately or unaffectionately—referred to as kooks." Stein herself "hasn't gone out of her way to help that reputation, with statements about vaccines and the dangers of wireless Internet." See Christopher Hooks, "What if the Green Party Stopped Being Kooky and Started Getting Real?" *Politico*, August 7, 2016.

should count. This means that votes should be cast for or against one of the two major candidates, even if the voter has a theoretical preference for a third-party candidate, unless the voter genuinely believes that neither major candidate is worse than the other. Even if a voter believes that the two major candidates present a choice of evils, that voter has the responsibility to vote for the lesser of the two evils—especially in a closely contested state—unless that vote would violate important principles. A protest vote for a third party in this election makes it more likely that the candidate the voter regards as the greater of the two evils will be elected.

I recall one of my first votes, in the presidential election of 1964. The choice was between Lyndon Johnson and Barry Goldwater. I detested them both, for different reasons: with Johnson it was a matter of character; with Goldwater it was his policies. I believed that Johnson was a crass, dishonest, opportunistic, manipulative southern power broker who had been elevated to the presidency by an assassin's bullet. I saw Goldwater as an honest, principled extremist whose warmongering might bring us closer to a nuclear confrontation with the Soviet Union. His mantra—"extremism in defense of liberty is no vice. Moderation in pursuit of justice is no virtue"—frightened me. At the beginning of the campaign, I was sure I couldn't vote for either candidate, but by the end, I decided that Goldwater posed a greater threat to our security than Johnson. So I held my nose and voted for Johnson, who turned out to be a great president on domestic issues, especially civil rights, but who foolishly and immorally expanded the war in Vietnam—a mixed bag. Who knows what Goldwater would have done in Vietnam.

In retrospect, I'm happy I voted for the lesser of the two evils rather than abdicating my responsibility.

Since the 1964 election, I have voted for many less than perfect candidates. Indeed, I have never been presented with a perfect candidate for whom to vote. Every one of them had flaws—personal, ideological, political—and yet in every case, one was better, or less bad, than the other. So I have always cast my vote for one of the major candidates. I have regretted a few of my votes in retrospect, but I have never regretted casting my ballot instead of staying home.

In the current presidential race, I have disagreements with both tickets on important substantive issues. I disagree with much of the Republican platform and with many of its candidates' positions, especially with regard to civil liberties and human rights. Although I am a lifelong Democrat and support nearly the entire Democratic Party's platform and the positions of its candidates, I disagree with my party and its candidates on the Iran nuclear deal, which they supported.

I was particularly distressed about Senator Tim Kaine's decision not to attend the speech of Israeli prime minister Benjamin Netanyahu when former Speaker of the House John Boehner invited him to deliver a speech to a joint session of Congress. He refused to listen to Netanyahu's arguments against the nuclear deal because he said that he disapproved of Netanyahu using the speech to bolster his election campaign in Israel. I was at the speech and I know that Netanyahu believed—and still believes—that the deal endangers Israel's security, and that he had a duty to try to stop it. In fact, opposition to the Iran deal was a bipartisan issue in Israel: Netanyahu's chief political rival, Isaac Herzog, also opposed the deal. And even if Netanyahu had gained some political advantage by speaking to Congress—which, as it turns out, he did not—he would surely not be the first democratically elected leader of an American ally to seek a political benefit at home for accepting an invitation to speak to Congress. By singling out the duly elected prime minister of Israel, Kaine contributed to an unhealthy environment in which Israel is often the victim of a double standard.

Kaine acknowledged that his decision not to attend Netanyahu's speech might cost him: "I'm not dumb. I know not going to the speech might make some folks mad with me—there would be a practical price, but I felt so strongly as a matter of principle that this was done in an entirely inappropriate way."[2] But many of us believe "strongly as a matter of principle" that the Iran deal for which he voted was "done in an entirely inappropriate way." The House voted against it and Kaine helped prevent the Senate from voting at all! So, yes, he is right: some folks, including me, are mad at him for refusing to attend Netanyahu's speech.* And that wrongheaded decision will be among the factors

---

* There was nothing inappropriate about Speaker Boehner inviting Prime Minister Netanyahu to address Congress. "Under the Constitution, the executive and legislative branches share responsibility for making and implementing important foreign-policy decisions. Congress has a critical role to play in scrutinizing the decisions of the president when these decisions involve national security, relationships with allies, and the threat of nuclear proliferation. Congress has every right to invite, even over the president's strong objection, any world leader or international expert who can assist its members in formulating appropriate responses to the current deal being considered with Iran regarding its nuclear-weapons program." Alan M. Dershowitz, "The Appalling Talk of Boycotting Netanyahu," *Wall Street Journal*, February 23, 2015.

I weigh in deciding whom to vote for and against. But it will not be the only factor. My decision will be based on what is best for America and for the world, including, but not limited to, Israel.

To be sure, I could never vote for a candidate who was anti-Israel, or who I believed would seriously endanger Israel's security, regardless of their views on other matters. If a truly anti-Israel candidate ran against a truly pro-Israel candidate who opposed the rights of women, gays, blacks, and other minorities, I would be presented with a terrible Hobson's choice. That may happen someday, if the Democratic Party—like the current Green Party—were to be taken over by hard-left Israel haters. But, thankfully, that is not my choice in this election. Moreover, that scenario is completely hypothetical, because any hard-left candidate who was truly anti-Israel and would endanger Israel's security would almost certainly be an extremist ideologue who supported other positions for which I could not vote: quasi censorship based on safe-space rhetoric, intersectional identity politics, nondemocratic confrontation tactics, and a state-control approach to the economy.

Both Hillary Clinton and Tim Kaine support Israel's security, as do President Barack Obama and Vice President Joe Biden. I disagree with some of their positions on the matter, as I have disagreed with every president regarding some of their positions on Israel. I also believe that Trump and Pence support a secure Israel, although I have no idea of where they—and especially Trump—stand on substantive issues regarding the conflict between Israel and its Arab neighbors. In this election, bipartisan support for Israel remains strong.

There is no excuse for anyone not to vote for or against

either Donald Trump or Hillary Clinton on November 8. The stakes are high. The issues that divide the candidates are clear. In the coming pages, I will lay out and analyze what I believe are the critical differences between the two candidates on ten fundamental issues that confront our nation and the world.

A Presidential Checklist

When I decide whom to vote for (or against) for president, I make a checklist of issues—in no particular order—that are important to me. Then I weigh them against each other. Here is my current checklist:

1. Who will best protect us from terrorism and other serious threats?

2. Who will keep America strong economically and militarily, while maintaining peace and avoiding unnecessary conflicts? Whose foreign policy best represents American values?

3. Who will best protect Israel's security and standing in the international community against military, terroristic, economic, political, and other threats, and who will do the most to try and bring about a fair and effective peace in the Middle East that assures Israel's security and the legitimate interests of its Palestinian and other neighbors?

4. Who will produce more stability and centrism in a world threatened by extremism?

5. Who will best protect our civil and constitutional rights?

ALAN DERSHOWITZ

6. Who will appoint competent and reasonable justices and judges?

7. Whose policies will best benefit the middle class and the economically disadvantaged?

8. Whose policies will better help reduce gun violence?

9. Which candidate is best positioned to address the immigration crisis?

10. Which candidate will be the best or worst overall president based on character, trust, tone, representation of American values, leadership skills, and the ability to confront unpredictable crises?

I will now go down the checklist and provide my own assessment of each major candidate by reference to the ten questions. Every reader will have a different assessment as to the pros and cons of each question and the relevant weight they would give to them. Many readers will have more or different questions on the checklist, but I suspect there will be considerable overlap with mine.

With a few exceptions, Clinton's policies represent a continuation of President Obama's, or a reversion to platforms embraced by previous Democratic administrations. They are generally heavy on detail and policy. Trump's proposals, by contrast, often lack detailed substance and are heavy on rhetoric—they often represent drastic departures from the established orthodoxies of both political parties. Perhaps their one unifying theme is that Trump says that he alone will "make American great again." Hopefully this brief summary will help voters decide whether that is indeed the case.

1) **Who will best protect us from terrorism and other serious threats?**

In light of the recent spate of terrorist attacks in Europe and the United States, perhaps the most pressing issue this election is how the candidates propose to protect American citizens from terrorism. Generally, these policies can be divided into two subcategories: the first relates to the prosecution of the war against ISIS in Syria and Iraq; the second deals with domestic policies that might prevent terrorist attacks in the United States.

Trump has promised to fight terrorism by using a wide array of aggressive military tactics to destroy ISIS in the Middle East, together with a series of domestic measures designed to deter "radical Islamic terrorism" in the United States. He summarized his approach to fighting terror at a rally in Ohio, when he said, "You have to fight fire with fire. We have to be so strong. We have to fight viciously. And violently because we're dealing with violent people viciously."[3]

The military tactics Trump has proposed include carpet bombing ISIS-controlled areas,* destroying ISIS-owned oil fields, and targeting the families of terrorists and ISIS members. He has also said that he would impose heavy sanctions on nations that support terrorism against the United States and its allies.

In contrast to the Obama administration, which has

---

* Although Trump later claimed that he had not used the term "carpet bomb," it is fair to say that this is what he essentially meant. At rallies, Trump has repeatedly said, "I would just bomb those suckers, and that's right, I'd blow up the pipes, I'd blow up the refineries, I'd blow up every single inch, there would be nothing left." Tim Hains, "Trump's Updated ISIS Plan: 'Bomb the Shit Out of Them,' Send in Exxon to Rebuild," RealClearPolitics, November 13, 2015.

painstakingly assembled a coalition of allies to fight ISIS in Syria and Iraq, Trump's vision of the war on terror seems more unilateral. He rarely mentions regional allies, and when he does, his attitude seems ambivalent at best: at times he has stated that he would "want to protect Saudi Arabia" and other regional allies; at others, he has stated that they're "going to have to help us economically" to ensure continued cooperation.

To combat terrorism domestically, Trump has proposed increasing surveillance of mosques, turning away Muslim refugees, halting all immigration from countries in the Middle East or countries "compromised by terrorism,"[4] and broadly loosening gun laws so that citizens can defend themselves against terrorists during an attack. He has also stated he would reauthorize the use of enhanced interrogation techniques like waterboarding suspected terrorists.

Although several of his proposals would violate international and domestic law—and several prominent members of the armed forces and CIA have stated they would not follow illegal directives (such as waterboarding and targeting civilians)—Trump has confidently stated that he could get our soldiers and law enforcement officials to implement them, and that he would appoint justices and judge who would authorize them.

Beyond revealing an alarming disrespect for the rule of law, Trump's approach raises two major questions: the first is whether his policies would actually decrease or increase terrorism. We cannot know for sure, but there is certainly a plausible argument that some of his extreme proposals—carpet bombing, waterboarding, surveilling mosques—might actually rehabilitate ISIS by cementing their narrative that the US and its allies are at war with the Muslim world, and by radicalizing Muslims both here in the Unites States and abroad. Nor is there any evidence that these proposals would even reduce terrorism in the short run. For example, there has been considerable debate over whether waterboarding is effective in eliciting truthful, real-time intelligence that is useful in preventing terrorism—in fact most intelligence experts, together with the members of the Senate Select Intelligence Committee, have concluded it does not. Equally, it is unclear how stemming immigration and the flow of refugees from the Middle East would prevent attacks that, until now, have been carried out for the most part by so-called homegrown terrorists both in Europe and the United States. FBI director James Comey worries that the defeat of ISIS abroad may well lead to an increase in terrorism at home because it will result in a "terrorist diaspora."[5]

What is clear is that Trump is prepared to violate existing international and domestic laws, as well as widely accepted principles of human rights, in his effort to stop terrorism—he is willing to do literally anything he thinks will keep Americans safe, and for some voters, that may be more important than actual policy specifics or compliance with the rule of law.

Clinton, on the other hand, has pledged to fight terrorism within the constraints of existing laws and principles. At times she has seemed more hawkish than the Obama administration—Clinton favored a more robust approach to Syria, for example, when the civil war escalated in 2015[6]—but generally she has promised to continue her predecessor's policies in the war on terror. She has pledged to continue working with our allies in the Middle East and in Europe to systematically degrade ISIS's territorial control in that region. In that effort, she is a strong supporter of air and drone strikes, but she rejects carpet bombing, targeting civilians, and waterboarding suspected terrorists, and she aims to utilize both military and diplomatic means in the quest to destroy ISIS in Iraq and Syria.

To prevent terrorism at home, she favors strengthening gun regulations so that suspected terrorists cannot so easily buy weapons, and working with Muslim communities in the United States to prevent the radicalization of young men who might be tempted to join ISIS. She strongly opposes Trump's proposed immigration restrictions based on religion, nationality, or ethnicity. These are largely the policies pursued by the Obama administration and embraced by the defense, military, and intelligence establishment. They have not prevented terrorist attacks altogether, but they have significantly diminished the capabilities of ISIS and al-Qaeda, and in the past year, they have successfully rolled back many of ISIS's territorial gains in Iraq. Nonetheless, Clinton's proposed policies do not pack the same rhetorical punch as Trump's "just bomb those suckers" strategies; to some voters, an emphasis on respecting the rule of law rings hollow when confronted with the barbarity of ISIS.

For those voters who care more about fighting terrorism by any means necessary than by doing so while complying with the rule of law and the principles of human rights, the question is purely empirical: Would Trump's proposals actually reduce or increase terrorism? We cannot know the answer to that question until and unless they are put into practice, but the fact that virtually the entirety of the defense and intelligence communities*—including staunch Republicans like Richard Armitage, Brent Scowcroft, and Robert Kagan—has endorsed Hillary Clinton should offer some comfort to those who want to see the war against terrorism conducted effectively within the rule of law.**

For those voters who seek to strike an appropriate balance between fighting terrorism and preserving liberty under the rule of law, the question is largely a moral one: Has Clinton struck the appropriate balance? Most centrist liberals think she largely has.

2) Who will keep America strong economically and militarily, while maintaining peace and avoiding unnecessary conflicts? Whose foreign policy best represents American values?

Both candidates have promised to "keep us strong and safe" (Clinton) or simply "strong again" (Trump) by advancing American defense and economic interests abroad. These generic statements, however, mean very different things to Trump and Clinton. Their statements on the campaign trail paint very different visions of America's role in the world.

---

* Most notably, fifty of the "most senior Republican national security officials, many of them former aides or cabinet members for President George W. Bush," signed a letter in which they stated that "none of us will vote for Trump," because he lacks the "character, values, and experience to be president." See David Sanger, "50 G.O.P Officials Warn Donald Trump Would Put Nation's Security 'At Risk,'" *New York Times*, August 8, 2016.

** Susan Collins, a Republican senator from Maine, also opposes Donald Trump on the grounds that he would make the world "more dangerous." Tal Kopan, "Susan Collins: Donald Trump Will Make the World 'More Dangerous,'" *CNN*, August 9, 2016.

Generally, Clinton has proposed a continuation of the Obama policies. She aims to continue President Obama's emphasis on multilateralism—one of her key policy planks is "stick with our allies" by strengthening "essential partnerships that are a unique source of America's strength." Similarly, she believes that diplomacy is an essential tool of projecting American power to solve "problems before they threaten us at home."

She favors partnerships with traditional allies in Europe, Asia, and the Middle East, and strongly supports US-led institutions like NATO—in fact, she affirms that "NATO is one of the best investments that America has ever made." Similarly, she views many of America's traditional antagonists with suspicion: she wants to deter Russian aggression in Europe and "stand up to Vladimir Putin"; she also aims to "hold China accountable" for violations of human rights, trade agreements, and territorial disputes. Nonetheless, like President Obama she also favors détente with Cuba and Iran, and she supports the Iran nuclear agreement, which she has promised to enforce aggressively.

Clinton's trade policies are equally nuanced: as first lady, she actively backed NAFTA, and as secretary of state she helped negotiate the Trans-Pacific Partnership. And while Clinton has walked back her support for the TPP, her choice of Tim Kaine—who had supported fast-track trade promotion to conclude the TPP in the Senate*—suggests some flexibility in her approach to trade.

---

* Although Kaine has voted for fast-track authority to expedite trade deals like TPP, right before the DNC he said he opposed the TPP. Dina Smeltz, "Did Tim Kaine Need to Flip His Position on the TPP to Win Sanders's Supporters? Nope." *Washington Post*, July 27, 2016.

She also believes that America should play a role in promoting values like democracy and human rights abroad, using both soft power and diplomacy, and, when necessary, military force. Indeed, one of the criticisms that Democrats often level against Clinton is that she is a hawk—while in the Senate, she voted to authorize the president to use military force in Iraq, and as secretary of state she was a proponent of the intervention in Libya. Clinton's stance on projecting American power seems slightly more hawkish than Obama's but with a similar focus on multilateralism.

Trump, by contrast, seems to reject almost every accepted orthodoxy of American foreign policy. Indeed, he has been consistently dismissive of "the career diplomats" and "the Washington ruling class" who in his view "are the people who got us into trouble." Generally, he feels that "what we are doing now isn't working." At times, however, Trump has been remarkably short on substance—shortly after announcing his presidential bid, for example, he told Bill O'Reilly that he was unwilling to discuss his foreign policy: "I'm not willing to tell you anything. And the reason I'm not is because if I run and win, I don't want them [US enemies] to know the game plan."

When he has been willing to share specifics, Trump has articulated his foreign policy approach in typically bombastic style. On the military, Trump has claimed that our current armed forces are a "disaster"[7] and that "there's nobody bigger or better at the military than I am." He claims that he would "find you a proper general, I would find the Patton or MacArthur, I would hit them [US enemies] so hard your head would spin." Exactly what that entails is open to debate, but this much is clear: unlike President

Obama and Secretary Clinton, he seems to have little regard for multilateralism. He has repeatedly suggested that as president, he would set conditions for defending NATO allies against attack. Similarly, he has argued that allies such as South Korea, Saudi Arabia, and Germany should pay for the protection provided by the US military. He also favors unwinding the Iran nuclear deal, which he has termed "a disgrace" and "one of the worst deals I have ever seen negotiated in my entire life."

But beyond reimposing and increasing sanctions—which would be very difficult to accomplish at this juncture, since our allies have given no indication that they would agree to a new sanctions regime—Trump has not told us what he would do to stop Iran from developing a nuclear arsenal if the deal were to be abrogated by the United States.

Like Clinton and Obama, Trump favors ending the embargo on Cuba. He has gone farther still in challenging the Republican foreign policy establishment by suggesting a rapprochement with Russia—indeed, Trump reportedly enjoys a friendly relationship with Vladimir Putin* and various Russian oligarchs who have invested in his commercial projects.[8] He has praised Putin for "bombing the hell out of ISIS" and has failed to condemn Russian intervention in Ukraine. During the Democratic convention, he went so far as to suggest—perhaps sarcastically—that Russia might help recover Hillary Clinton's missing emails!

---

* However, it is not clear how much of that is true. Trump used to boast that he had a friendly relationship with Putin, saying, "I got to know him very well because we were both on *60 Minutes*." Later he had to revise the story, admitting, "I never met Putin. I don't know who Putin is." S. V. Date, "Trump Used to Say He Was Pals With Putin. Now He Says They Never Met," *Huffington Post*, July 27, 2016.

In terms of economic strength, Trump has promised to rescind trade deals that do not represent a "win" for America. These include NAFTA, the TPP, and, apparently, existing bilateral trade deals with countries like China, because they promote "stupid trade." However, like with so many of his proposals, Trump has failed to define what "smart trade" or a "trade win" would represent, much less how he would improve existing agreements to benefit American consumers and manufacturers.

Finally, Trump has effectively acknowledged that he will not seek to export our democratic and other positive values to other countries. He has stated that the attempts by the George W. Bush administration to do so in the Middle East were a mistake, and that, generally, the US has no business criticizing other countries' governments, especially if they are our allies. In fact, Trump has been remarkably sympathetic to autocrats, such as Turkey's Recep Tayyip Erdoğan, Russia's Vladimir Putin, and Hungary's Viktor Orbán—who in turn seem sympathetic to him.

In general, Trump's foreign policy seems to be channeling an underlying emotion felt by a great number of voters—that the United States is no longer the dominant superpower that it once was—and Trump's rhetorical flourishes seem to speak to this sentiment. Trump's vision pits America against the rest of the world and promises that only Trump will make American "win" and "win big." His slogan of "America First" suggests little concern for the rest of the world. Certainly, Trump seems more predisposed to take unilateral military action if he feels it will help America "win."

Some people believe that Trump's thin skin, peevishness, and need for revenge might incline him toward knee-jerk military action. I don't necessarily agree, though one can never be sure. Clinton, by contrast, represents a known quantity. While she has no direct experience with the military, as secretary of state she was involved in military decisions, such as the killing of Osama Bin Laden, but she was also tangentially involved in the tragic events at Benghazi. She is perhaps too hawkish for some Democrats, but equally, she is too dovish for many Republicans—many of them, and some pro-Israel Democrats, feel that she made a serious mistake by supporting the Iran nuclear agreement.

The United States must remain a force for positive change in the world—we have both the moral authority and a moral obligation to promote human rights and to support nations that espouse liberal democratic governance. Trump's pseudo-isolationism runs counter to this view of the world. But my comparative analysis of Trump's foreign policy stances versus Clinton's also depends on the next two items on the checklist: Who will protect Israel's security? And which candidate will better stabilize an international environment that is increasingly fraught by extremism?

3) Who will best protect Israel's security and standing in the international community against military, terroristic, economic, political, and other threats, and who will do the most to try and bring about a fair and effective peace in the Middle East that assures Israel's security and the legitimate interests of its Palestinian and other neighbors?

There will be much debate, especially within the pro-Israel community, about which candidate will best protect Israel's security and do the most to bring about a fair and effective peace between Israel and its neighbors. Little is known about Trump's views on the specifics of the Mideast conflict. We know he regards the Iran deal as "terrible" and that he would seek to expand sanctions against Iran. He has also criticized the Obama administration for allowing the relationship with Israeli prime minister Netanyahu to deteriorate so severely.

However, some of his statements regarding the Israeli-Palestinian conflict have been somewhat discomforting. Trump has repeatedly stated that he believes that he could negotiate a deal between the two parties, but that in order to do so he would need to assume a neutral position between the Israelis and the Palestinians. As with many of Trump's foreign policy positions, it's unclear exactly what that would entail. Certainly, Senator Rubio was not impressed by his lack of specificity: "He thinks a Palestine and Israel settlement is a real estate deal. The Palestinians are not a real estate deal, Donald."

Even more disturbingly, Trump has sometimes lurched into the realm of dog-whistle anti-Semitism by half-heartedly courting the support of white-nationalist bigots. In June, for example, Trump re-tweeted an image first posted on a white-supremacist message board featuring a pile of cash and a Star of David, together with a picture of Hillary Clinton.[9] In May, Trump refused for several days to disavow the endorsement of the leader of the KKK, David Duke, claiming: "I don't know anything about David Duke."[10] Trump also revealed a penchant for stereotyping Jews during a speech to Republican Jewish donors in New York.[11] Nonetheless, I have little doubt that a President Trump would defend the nation-state of the

Jewish people—he has made supporting Israel a central plank of his foreign policy platform, and has surrounded himself with Israel-friendly advisors.[12]

Clinton's views on Israel are more detailed and nuanced. She supports Israel's right to defend its citizens against rocket attacks, terror tunnels, and other forms of terrorism, and favors maintaining or increasing Israel's qualitative military advantage over its potential enemies. She advocates the two-state solution that will assure Israel's security and opposes Israeli settlement building on the West Bank. She supported the Iran deal, though she said she would demand full compliance by Iran. Her foreign policy platform calls for full support of Israel's ability to defend itself, including by maintaining existent arms agreements, and by opposing "efforts to marginalize Israel on the world stage." Clinton's record of standing up for Israel both as first lady, as a senator from New York, and as Secretary of State is generally quite good.* While I disagree with her evaluation of the Iran nuclear agreement during her tenure as secretary of state, I trust her when she says that she aims to "deepen our unshakable commitment to Israel's security"—indeed, she has stood firm in her unwavering support for Israel despite significant pressure from the left of the Democratic Party.

The important point is that in this election, both candidates and their vice presidential running mates have

---

* Clinton's receipt, while she was secretary of state, of emails from Max Blumenthal—a virulently anti-Israel activist, author, and journalist, whose writings sometimes cross the line into anti-Semitism—has caused concern among some voters. Max's father, Sydney Blumethal, has long been a close Clinton associate, and he forwarded his son's writings to Clinton. See Allison Kaplan Sommer, "Do Anti-Israel Emails from Hillary's Inner Circle Show Her True Colors?", *Haaretz*, January 15, 2016.

expressed strong support for Israel's security, thus keeping it a bipartisan issue. That said, I recognize that reasonable people could disagree as to who would better protect Israel's security and seek a peaceful resolution of the decades-long conflict. Trump's substantive views are less known than Clinton's. For those who seek more certainty and predictability, Clinton may be a better bet. Trump might earn the votes of those who want to see a change in the status quo without knowing the precise nature of the change.

What Israel fears most is an unstable and unpredictable world in which the influence of extremists grows. Both the Jewish people and its nation-state thrive on centrist politics of the kind represented by Clinton and discussed under the next heading.

4) Who will produce more stability and centrism in a world threatened by extremism?

This is the most important issue in the 2016 election, since instability around the world is growing and extremist parties and leaders—both hard right and hard left—are increasing their influence.

There can be little doubt that Clinton is more likely than Trump to be a force for stability in the world. Indeed, as discussed above, Trump is running to shake up America's relationship with the international community. He wants to change our relationship with NATO, to change our trade deals, to break up the European Union, to revisit the nuclear deal with Iran, to build a wall between Mexico and the United States, to strike a different balance between our support for Israel and the Palestinians, to challenge China's monetary policies, and to befriend

Russia at the expense of our traditional allies in Europe.

Without going into the merits or demerits of these changes—and there are perhaps merits to some—it is clear that his election would have a destabilizing effect on the world. Those are his express goals. He makes no secret of them. He wants to shake up the world. He wants to put "America first"—above the needs of international stability. This plan raises several important questions: Is world stability, rather than instability, good or bad for the United States? Would an unstable world—economically, politically, militarily, diplomatically—really put America first? Or is it to our selfish advantage—that is Trump's criterion—to maintain stability, even in the face of an imperfect status quo? With so many European and other countries moving toward extremism in their politics, is this the right time for such a shake-up, or would instability increase the trend toward political extremism?

The answers to these and other questions are anything but certain. And that is the real danger. Trump's election—indeed his nomination—risks uncertainty, unpredictability, and instability. We simply don't know what we would be getting with a Trump presidency, because there is no record of government service, no clear set of policies, and no consistent theme, other than change for the sake of change. "We will win and win big" is a bumper sticker, a college cheer, a boast. It is not a program. Viewing our relationship with the rest of the world—including our allies—as a zero-sum game, in which every time we "win, and win big," someone loses, may be a good strategy for sports or business, but it is not necessarily the best way to assure a stable world. Planning for the future becomes difficult, if not impossible, under this approach.

There is certainly a need for change in the world, and some of Trump's substantive ideas—to the extent that they are understandable and coherent—may well serve America's interests, but the package he represents threatens the stability of the world precisely at a time when that is most needed. As David Leonhardt, an op-ed columnist for the *New York Times*, put it, "Were [Trump] to win, the country could enter a period of instability few of us have known."[13]

Clinton represents the polar opposite of Trump on the issue of world stability. She is a known commodity around the planet, having served as secretary of state for four years, as first lady for eight years, and as a senator from New York for eight years. She has been in the public eye for more than a quarter century, which is much of the adult lives of world leaders and citizens. Her policies, positions, and personality are well known and generally respected. She is more trusted abroad than at home, but that is true of many world leaders. She, too, has promised change, but the changes she has promised are incremental, gradual, predictable, and widely acceptable. She is certainly viewed as a centrist, who supports evolution rather than revolution, liberalism rather than radicalism, rapprochement rather than confrontation, globalization rather than xenophobia or parochialism.

These are among the reasons why she is the overwhelming favorite of people around the world—both liberals and conservatives—and why a Trump victory is so frightening to so many of our allies. But being more popular abroad than at home is not necessarily a prescription for electoral victory. Tip O'Neill's mantra that "All politics is local" may be somewhat anachronistic in our age of globalization, but Trump is running against globalization and in favor of putting America first.

So for those voters who agree that America should be put first, the major question is whether the likely instability resulting from a Trump victory will help or hurt America. For voters who take a broader view of American responsibility to the world, there is little question that a Clinton victory would produce greater stability in a world that is becoming destabilized by the growing influence of extremes in politics.

5) Who will best protect civil and constitutional rights?

Much like President Obama, Clinton supports civil rights and embraces a vision of the Constitution that provides protections for racial, ethnic, and religious minorities, as well as other groups who are subject to discrimination. Indeed, civil rights has been one of the defining threads of Clinton's political career.

Despite being born into a family of staunch Republicans, she defected to the Democratic Party in college, largely due to Republican opposition to civil rights. Her graduation speech at Wellesley made headlines in 1969 for championing activism on civil rights issues, and as a young lawyer she went undercover to help expose illegally segregated schools in Alabama.

Her policy platform reflects her commitment to these issues: she is in favor of affirmative action and other measures geared toward promoting racial equality both in the education system and the workforce. Similarly, she favors legislation to remedy the gender wage gap and has made women's rights a cornerstone of her campaign. She has always supported a woman's right to choose an abortion—and in this election cycle she was the first Democratic presidential candidate to call for the repeal of the Hyde Amendment, which bans the use of federal Medicaid to pay for abortions.[14]

On gay marriage, Clinton's views have evolved considerably, as they have for most of her generation of Democrats: she stood by her husband when, as president, he signed the 1996 Defense of Marriage Act. And although she supported same-sex unions as early as 1999, she opposed same-sex marriages when she ran for Senate in New York and during her first presidential run in 2008. Today her platform unambiguously supports LGBT rights, including same-sex marriage; Clinton also supports anti-discrimination legislation for gay and transgender individuals.

As regards other constitutional protections, Clinton has espoused the centrist Democratic party line. She generally supports the First Amendment, but also believes in narrow exceptions necessary to protect national security. She has also appeared sympathetic to efforts by Muslim nations at the UN to ban expressions they deem offensive, but, in a domestic context, she has defended the rights of individuals to express offensive and even blasphemous ideas. For example, following the release of the provocative video "The Innocence of Muslims," just before the attack on the consulate in Benghazi, Secretary Clinton stated:

> I know it is hard for some people to understand why
> the United States cannot or does not just prevent these
> kinds of reprehensible videos from ever seeing the light
> of day.... Even if it were possible, our country does have a
> long tradition of free expression which is enshrined in our

Constitution and our law, and we do not stop individual citizens from expressing their views no matter how distasteful they may be.[15]

She has struck a moderate tone on Fourth Amendment protections. In the 1990s she and her husband pushed anti-crime legislation designed to empower law enforcement and to fight the perceived drug epidemic—since then she has moved to the left, and recognizes that her husband's administration overstepped with the 1994 crime bill. As regards capital punishment, she is not in favor of abolishing the death penalty completely—she only wants to see it applied in rare and limited cases.

While Clinton's views on civil rights and constitutional protections are largely in line with the liberal centrist consensus that has developed over the course of the Obama presidency, Trump is somewhat of an apostate Republican on several issues. On gay marriage, for example, Trump has long espoused positions far to the left of many of his primary opponents, and certainly to the evangelical Christian base, who have been among his core of supporters. As early as 2000, Trump declared that he supported gay anti-discrimination laws and the repeal of "don't ask, don't tell," and he was on the record as favoring "a very strong domestic-partnership law that guarantees gay people the same legal protections and rights as married people."[16]

Similarly, this election cycle he has stuck to relatively moderate positions regarding transgender rights. With regard to the transgender bathroom controversy in North Carolina, Trump argued that "there have been very few complaints the way it is. People... should use the bathroom that they feel is appropriate."[17] Later he backtracked, stating: "I think that local communities and states should make the decision. The federal government should not be involved."[18]

On abortion, Trump has also repeatedly changed positions. Before launching his political career, he supported a women's right to choose. Since then, he has tacked hard to the right. In an interview with Chris Matthews in Green Bay, Wisconsin, he famously declared that there should be some form of punishment for women who receive abortions, and for doctors who perform them.[19] Even staunch Republicans were dismayed by this pronouncement, and Trump has since sought to moderate his position.

Many commentators seized on Trump's abortion snafu to suggest that he hadn't put a great deal of thought into the issue and that he was merely offering an answer that he thought would please the Republican base. This may well be the case. Trump has not put social issues front and center; he has generally steered clear of the "culture wars" that defined Republican politics since the late 1990s.

Trump's positions on other constitutional protections, particularly those related to the First Amendment, will concern civil libertarians. He has suggested that he would loosen libel laws so that he could sue media organizations; he has argued that activist groups like Black Lives Matter should be investigated and shut down; and he has argued that Muslims should be banned from immigrating to the United States.

These proposals may violate the First Amendment protections on speech, association, and religion, respectively, and even though Trump has subsequently modified them, they reflect an emphasis on tough ends rather than constitutional means. This view is also reflected in Trump's discussion of crime and policing: inevitably, he favors strong police tactics and rarely, if ever, discusses the legal safeguards afforded to defendants by the Constitution.

Trump seems equally unconcerned about constitutional protections against race discrimination. Speaker of the House Paul Ryan characterized his suggestion that a federal judge could not perform his responsibilities because of his ethnicity "the textbook definition of racism." His pronouncement that many Mexican immigrants are rapists and his reluctance to distance himself from bigots like David Duke similarly reflect an animus toward ethnic minorities that augurs poorly for the vigorous protection of civil rights.

With regard to the constitutional issue of separation of church and state, neither candidate is perfect, because most citizens want to see more religion in government. Both candidates proclaim their belief in God and their religious affiliation, as if these factors qualify them for elected office. Their vice presidential running mates have emphasized their faiths even more than the presidential candidates. All four candidates disregard Jefferson's admonition to keep one's religious views private and his assertion that one's beliefs or disbeliefs in religion are irrelevant to morality or qualification to govern.* That said, Trump and Pence and the party they represent support prayers in public schools, which promote divisions along religious lines. During his campaign, Trump has also made it a point to question the sincerity of one of his opponents' religious

---

* Thomas Jefferson famously said, "Our civil rights have no dependence on our religious opinions any more than our opinions in physics or geometry."

beliefs.[20] That too should give pause to everyone who is worried about widening religious divisions in our country. Trump and Pence also support giving tax exemptions to churches, synagogues, and mosques that espouse overtly political views from the pulpit. On the issue of church and state, Clinton is less bad than Trump, though neither passes the Jefferson test.

There can be little doubt that for voters who care about civil and constitutional rights: the choice of Hillary Clinton is clear. It certainly seems clear to most African-Americans, Latinos, women, LGBTQ people, Muslims, and others who have long been denied equal protection of the laws.

6) Who will appoint competent and reasonable justices and judges?

With the Republican leadership's stubborn refusal to confirm President Obama's Supreme Court nominee, Judge Merrick Garland, to succeed the late justice Antonin Scalia, and three liberal justices in their late seventies or early eighties, it is likely that the next president will be able to make a number of decisive judicial appointments and change the ideological makeup of the high court for decades to come.

Hillary Clinton has stated that she would nominate judges like Justice Sonia Sotomayor, whose Hispanic background and underprivileged upbringing add a much-needed perspective to the court. Clinton has also said that she would impose litmus tests on abortion and campaign finance; in other words, she would only appoint someone who would uphold *Roe v. Wade* and overturn *Citizens United*.

Trump, by contrast, has said he would appoint judges in the mold of Justice Scalia. Given Trump's tenuous grasp on the basic principles of our legal system, many conservatives questioned whether he had actually given any thought to the issue of judicial appointments. Eventually, Trump released a list of eleven judges whom he said he would consider nominating to the Supreme Court; all of them were white, conservative, pro-life judges, and some had a record of curtailing women's and LGBT rights. Trump has not spoken of a litmus test for appointments to the Supreme Court, but his list of potential appointments perhaps suggests one.

So what can we expect from a Trump nominee versus a Clinton nominee? History tells us that judges tend to rule according to the ideology of the president who appointed them, despite several recent outliers, such as retired justice David Souter, and to some extent Justice Anthony Kennedy. In essence, this means that Trump appointees would perpetuate a conservative agenda—limiting a woman's right to choose, lowering the wall of separation between church and state, striking down gun regulations, curtailing civil rights protections for LGBT Americans, and curtailing other basic rights.

Conversely, were Hillary Clinton to make the next two or three judicial appointments, we may see the most liberal Supreme Court since the Warren court. Of course, one can never be certain how a particular Supreme Court justice will vote. President Eisenhower famously called his appointment of Justices William Brennan and Earl Warren the biggest mistakes of his presidency.

If the recent trend continues and justices (who have constitutionally guaranteed life tenure) are being appointed when they are fairly young—Justices Clarence Thomas and John Roberts were forty-three and fifty respectively when they were appointed to the highest court—the next president's agenda will have an imprint on our nation long after her or his time in the Oval Office. So the stakes to elect someone who will nominate competent and reasonable justices and judges could not be any higher.

For those who want more Justice Scalias, the choice is Trump. For those who want more Justice Sotomayors, the choice is Clinton.

7) Whose policies will best benefit the middle class and the economically disadvantaged?

Here we have a classic conflict between the Democratic and Republican approaches to helping the poor (with the exception of Trump's opposition to free trade deals).

Democrats traditionally believe in helping the economically disadvantaged directly with higher wages, lower taxes on the poor and middle class (with higher taxes for the wealthy), better public education for poor school districts, free public higher education for those who can't afford current tuitions, better health care for the poor, and other direct subsidies and transfer of wealth from the rich to the poor.

Clinton has generally embraced this approach—unlike her husband, who felt compelled by the political environment in the 1990s to pursue relatively moderate fiscal policies. She has steered to the left on issues like the minimum wage, Wall Street regulation, health care, and public education. Her platform calls for strengthening the Affordable Care and Dodd-Frank acts, and for raising taxes on the wealthy. In this regard, Bernie Sanders has acted as an anchor to her left—his unexpected primary challenge forced Clinton to commit to a fifteen-dollar minimum wage, to walk back her support for free trade agreements like the TPP, and to come up with a generous college tuition plan.

Republicans traditionally reject these approaches and believe in the "rising tide" and "trickle-down" theories under which helping big businesses, lowering taxes on the wealthy, and improving the general economy are the best ways of helping the middle class and the poor. Trump generally subscribes to this approach to the economy. His tax plan calls for cuts across the board, but he has steered the right of the Republican establishment by arguing for the abolition of the federal minimum wage. He also favors Wall Street deregulation—indeed, he has pledged to dismantle Dodd-Frank because the law "made it impossible for bankers to function."[21] Similarly, he vowed to repeal and replace Obamacare with a single-payer health care system but then backtracked and proposed instituting a private system with free-market principles.

However, in typical fashion—and unlike previous nominees like Romney and McCain—Trump has sometimes eschewed traditional Republican talking points on the economy. In particular, Trump has displayed a proclivity for protectionist economic policies—indeed, he seems to believe that limiting foreign imports via tariffs is an effective way to restore American manufacturing jobs. Many prominent Republicans and independents have therefore denounced a Trump presidency. Hank Paulson, former CEO of Goldman Sachs and treasury secretary under George W. Bush, wrote:

When Trump assures us he'll do for the United States what he's done for his businesses, that's not a promise—it's a threat. The tactics he has used in running his business wouldn't work in running a truly successful company, let alone the most powerful nation on Earth.... The average American household income is roughly $10,000 higher because of the postwar expansion of trade. Because of trade, we add jobs and foster innovation and competitiveness.... It is wrong to tell the American people that we can turn back the clock and win.... The policies Trump endorses would destroy, not save, US jobs.

Similarly, former Republican and mayor of New York Michael Bloomberg endorsed Clinton, while acknowledging her imperfections. Instead of effusive praise for her, Bloomberg focused on Trump's inadequacies:

Given my background, I've often encouraged business leaders to run for office because many of them share that same pragmatic approach to building consensus, but not all. Trump says he wants to run the nation like he's run his business? God help us.

Trump has frequently boasted about his wealth and argued that his experience in business would make up for his dearth of experience in politics. Those who tend to assume that the economy is better served if a Republican and businessman sits in the Oval Office should be reminded of Paulson's and Bloomberg's warnings when they cast their ballots in November.

Reasonable voters will disagree as to which of these approaches is best for the poor. I don't know the answer, though I generally support the more direct and immediate approach of the Democrats. Voters who support the Republicans' approach may be inclined to check this box in favor of Trump, although laissez-faire Republicans may be put off by his willingness to meddle with the free market.

8) Whose policies will better help reduce gun violence?

Much as with their economic platforms, Trump and Clinton largely follow their respective party lines with respect to reducing gun violence.

While Clinton promised in her nomination acceptance speech that she is "not here to take away your guns," Clinton is in favor of a wide range of gun control measures, including banning the sales of automatic weapons and expanding background checks; she also favors laws that stop domestic abusers, individuals on the terrorist watch list, and the mentally ill from purchasing firearms. Generally, Clinton "believes weapons of war have no place on our streets"* and that "you shouldn't be able to exploit loopholes and evade criminal background checks" to buy weapons. She has argued that increased gun-control legislation is critical to reducing deaths from gun violence and also a matter of national security, to prevent attacks like the one that occurred in San Bernardino, California, in December 2015.

Trump is her polar opposite. In his words, "I'm a big Second Amendment person." He has repeatedly advocated loosening gun regulations, arguing that a more widely

---

* I believe that the president, as commander-in-chief of our armed forces, may well have the constitutional authority to have the Department of Defense categorize fully automatic machine guns, for example, as military weapons, and to preclude their sale to civilians.

armed populace would reduce deaths from gun violence. Generally, Trump subscribes to the NRA line that "the only person who stops a bad guy with a gun is a good guy with a gun." However, Trump has at times gone even farther than the NRA. In June, following the terrorist attack at an Orlando nightclub, for example, he argued that people should be allowed to carry guns in bars, only to be sharply rebuked by NRA spokesman Wayne LaPierre: "I don't think you should have firearms where people are drinking."

More recently, Trump warned a rally in North Carolina that Clinton wants to "essentially abolish the Second Amendment." He claimed that it would be a "horrible day" for gun owners if Clinton were elected president and had the power to appoint a justice favorably disposed towards gun-control legislation: "If she gets to pick her judges, nothing you can do, folks." The crowd began to boo and shout, and then Trump added the following words: "Although the Second Amendment people—maybe there is, I don't know."[22] In analyzing the impact of this ambiguous statement on viewers and listeners, it must be recalled that many "Second Amendment people" believe that the purpose of the Second Amendment is to give the people the means to overthrow the government if it becomes tyrannical.[23] For those who believe this—and there are many—Trump's statement was more than a "dog whistle," it was a license to stop the tyranny that they believe would follow from a Clinton presidency with a Supreme Court that might overrule or limit the Heller decision, which interpreted the Second Amendment as providing a personal right to "keep and bear arms," rather than a restriction on the power of the federal government to impose limits on a well-regulated militia.* Whatever may have been Trump's intention in uttering these words, he surely must have realized that some unhinged followers might be incited to consider assassination as a way to do something to stop Clinton from taking away their guns. Presidential candidates must consider the impact their words may have on others.

Ultimately, the question is whether the Clinton-Brady approach or the Trump-NRA approach is more likely to reduce gun violence. Although there is some academic debate on this empirical issue,[24] I think the evidence comparing gun violence in America to other countries that have effective gun control makes it clear that Clinton should get the votes of those who are most concerned about reducing gun violence.

9) Which candidate is best positioned to address the immigration crisis?

Trump has made dealing with illegal immigration the cornerstone of his campaign. Indeed, there is probably no single issue on which the candidates can be more easily separated, in terms of both rhetoric and policy.

In his announcement speech, Trump notoriously called Mexican illegal immigrants rapists and murderers. He also suggested that the US build a wall across the US-Mexico border and have Mexico pay for it. He wants to increase border control and also end birthright citizenship, thereby denying children who are born in the US to illegal immigrants US citizenship—a change that could probably

---

* The full text of the Second Amendment reads: "A well regulated militia being necessary to the security of a free state, the right of the people to keep and bear arms shall not be infringed."

not be accomplished without a constitutional amendment.

On the issue of refugees, Trump has wobbled considerably. At the beginning of his campaign, Trump spoke in favor accepting Syrian refugees, arguing that "on a humanitarian basis you have to.... They are living in hell, and something has to be done." Later in the campaign he revised his stance, calling for a ban on immigrants seeking refuge from terrorism. He criticized Europe for accepting so many Syrian refugees, saying that he would have "absolutely no problem looking Syrian children in the face" and telling them to "go home." And he called for a ban on all Muslim immigrants to the United States "until our country's representatives can figure out what is going on."[25]

As for regular work visas, Trump has flip-flopped several times during his campaign. For his Florida golf resorts, Trump used—and continues to use—the H-1B program, and supported bringing and keeping highly skilled workers to the country. But he also said he would like to end the H-1B program because he believes it is being abused to the detriment of American workers.* It is not clear where Trump really stands on this issue. When asked at the first presidential GOP debate about his inconsistent answers, he admitted, "I'm changing. I'm changing."[26]

Hillary Clinton's positions on immigration, by contrast, have been a model of consistency. Ever since serving as senator for New York, Clinton has favored comprehensive immigration reform that would address existing

---

* While he was on the campaign trail and declared his intention to end this guest worker program, Trump continued to file for visas for seventy-eight foreign workers in his Florida resorts, claiming he couldn't find enough American workers to do the jobs. Jessica Garrison, Jeremy Singer-Vine, and Ken Bensinger, "Trump Seeks More Foreign Guest Workers for His Companies," BuzzFeed, July 27, 2016.

problems with the high-skill labor flow, border security, and so-called illegal immigration.

Most controversially for many conservatives, Clinton's immigration platform calls for the humane enforcement of immigration laws—only "those individuals who pose a violent threat to public safety" should be deported—and for some type of pathway to citizenship for the large undocumented population already living in the United States.

Clinton has promised to introduce some form of comprehensive immigration reform legislation to Congress within the first hundred days of her presidency. Her campaign has stated that "if Congress keeps failing to act on comprehensive immigration reform, Hillary will enact a simple system for those with sympathetic cases"—including "parents of DREAMers" and "those with a history of service and contribution to their communities." Generally, Clinton views immigration favorably and has sought to garner support from the growing Hispanic community in the United States. By appointing Tim Kaine as her running mate, she has doubled down on this approach—Kaine spent many of his first appearances on the campaign trail arguing (often in Spanish) that immigration reform is one of the great tasks facing the next administration.

As regards refugees, Clinton has largely followed the lead of the Obama administration: she has supported accepting Syrian refugees—indeed, in September 2015, she called for the US to admit as many as sixty-five thousand over the course of the next year, arguing that the additional vetting measures imposed by the Department of Homeland Security are sufficient to address any potential security concerns.

For those who fear immigration and seek to reduce the

number of Mexicans and Muslims allowed in this country, the argument for Trump is clear. For those who favor a more balanced and humane approach, the argument for Clinton is equally clear.

10) Which candidate will be the best or worst overall president based on character, trust, tone, representation of American values, leadership skills, and the ability to confront unpredictable crises?

The final and summary question for every voter is: Who will be the best or worst overall president?

Each voter will have to make his or her own judgment on these highly subjective issues.

There can be little doubt that Clinton will better export American values around the world. Trump has as much as acknowledged that he will not seek to impart our democratic and other positive values to other countries. He has pitted America against the rest of the world and said he will make America "win" and "win big." He is campaigning on a slogan of "America First" and seems to care little about the rest of the world. Clinton is a globalist who believes that America should lead by example. Clinton will clearly represent American values around the world far better than Trump.

Neither candidate scores high on the trust factor. Both have been accused, fairly or unfairly, of taking liberties with the truth. Trust is a personal factor that each voter will have to decide for themselves. Based on their history and track records, I trust Trump less than I do Clinton.

On the issue of tone, there is little doubt that Trump has been extraordinarily negative, mocking the disabled, referring to a woman's menstrual cycle and a man's penis size, using racist, sexist, and scatological language—and in general being crass and bombastic. For voters who favor such "direct" talk, the choice of Trump may be suitable. For those of us who seek a president from whom our children and grandchildren can learn good manners and basic decency, and who is more presidential in tone, the choice of Clinton should seem obvious.

Leadership skills and the ability to confront the unexpected are difficult to evaluate, except by reference to the experience and history of each candidate. Trump's experience has been in business and on television. Clinton's has been in governance and public service. In business, failure to anticipate and deal with unpredictable crises can be covered by resorting to bankruptcy protection, as Trump has shown us. In television, they can be covered by reshooting the scene, as I'm sure Trump did many times. In governance, there are no bankruptcy protections or reshoots. There are no do-overs. Clinton has a long—if sometimes controversial—record of dealing with crises. She is the leader I would trust most to deal effectively with the inevitable 3:00 a.m. call.

On the overall question of who would make a better—and certainly a less dangerous—president, I have little doubt. That's why I will vote for Hillary Clinton on November 8, 2016.

Conclusion

This is the strangest presidential election in my memory. Despite the polls, it is utterly unpredictable. Polling is incapable of accurately predicting the outcome of elections in which so many voters are unaroused by either candidate, angry at the system that produced them, resentful, emotional, negative, frightened, and themselves unpredictable. Many unaroused voters now say they won't vote at all, or will vote for a third-party candidate. They may, of course, end up voting for one of the two major candidates when Election Day comes around.

This may depend on whether the Johnson-Weld ticket does well enough in the polls to be included in the presidential and vice presidential debates. The rules require that a third-party candidate reach 15 percent in five national polls. This number is difficult to achieve because many of the polls do not include third-party candidates. But it is not impossible, and if it were to occur, and if the Johnson-Weld ticket outperformed or held its own against Clinton and Trump, then people who had decided not to vote or who couldn't make up their minds might cast ballots for the Libertarian candidates. It is unlikely that the Stein/Baraka ticket will be included in the debates or that it will garner any significant number of voters in key states.

The bottom line is that in a bizarre election like this one—with so many variables and so much emotion—polls may well under- or overpredict votes for the two major candidates.

Think about the vote on Brexit. Virtually all the polls[1]—including exit polls that asked voters *whom they had voted for*—got it wrong. The financial markets got it wrong. The bookies got it wrong.[2] The 2016 presidential election is more like the Brexit vote in many ways than it is like prior presidential elections. Both Brexit and this presidential election involve raw emotion, populism, anger, nationalism (Britain First, America First), class division, and other factors that distort accuracy in polling. So anyone who thinks they know who will be the next president of the United States is deceiving themselves.

To be sure, the Electoral College vote is sometimes less difficult to predict than the popular vote, because it generally turns on a handful of closely contested critical states, such as Ohio, Florida, Pennsylvania, and Virginia. But in this election, there could be surprises in states that are usually secure for one party or the other. So even the electoral vote will be more difficult to predict than in previous elections.

One reason for this unique unpredictability is the unique unpredictability of Donald Trump himself. No one really knows what he will say or do between now and the election. His position on important issues may change. Live televised debates will not allow him to rely on a teleprompter, as he largely did in his acceptance speech. He may once again become a loose cannon, as he was during the live primary debates. Indeed, since I completed my initial draft of this book, Trump insulted a Gold Star mother, had a crying baby removed from a rally, made an incendiary statement about "Second Amendment people" and more. This may gain him votes, or it may lose him votes. Trump told Sean Hannity that he was benefitting from the controversy surrounding his "second amendment people" statement: "it's a good thing for me."[3] When it comes to Donald Trump, nobody can tell. Few, if any, pundits accurately predicted how far Trump would get when he first entered the race. When it comes to Donald Trump, the science of polling seems inadequate to the task.

Hillary Clinton is more predictable, but her past actions may produce unpredictable results, as they did when FBI director Comey characterized her conduct with regard to her emails as "extremely careless." It is also possible that more damaging information may come from WikiLeaks or other such sources.*

Another unpredictable factor that may impact the election is whether there are terrorist attacks in the lead-up to the voting. Islamic extremists would almost certainly like to see Trump beat Clinton, because they believe a Trump presidency would result in the kind of instability on which they thrive. If ISIS attacks American targets in late October, that could turn some undecided voters in favor of the candidate who says he will do anything to stop terrorism.

Although there are no perfect analogies, the election

---

* I have consulted professionally with Julian Assange and his London lawyers, but not about this issue.

of Benjamin Netanyahu as prime minister of Israel in 1996 may provide some historical context. In the run-up to that election, some polls had Shimon Peres ahead of Netanyahu by double digits. Then Hamas started to blow up buses in Jerusalem and Tel Aviv. This caused some Israelis to vote for Netanyahu, who was perceived as tougher on terrorism. Whether it actually impacted the election can never be known for sure, since there were many other factors in play. But it is clear that Hamas timed its terrorist attacks to have maximum impact on that election.[4]

It is important that this issue be openly discussed in advance so as to blunt the impact of any terrorist attacks on American voting. We must not allow terrorists to determine who will be the next president of the US. If there are terrorist attacks, voters should understand that changing their vote plays into the hands of terrorists and will only encourage them to try to influence future elections by timing such attacks.

A final reason why this election is so unpredictable is because the voter turnout is unpredictable. The "Bernie or bust" crowd is threatening to stay home or vote for the Green Party. Young voters may do here what they did in Great Britain: many failed to vote in the Brexit referendum and then regretted their inaction when it became clear that if they had voted in the same proportion as older voters, Brexit would likely have been defeated. Some Clinton supporters worry that black voters who voted in large numbers for Barack Obama may cast fewer votes for Clinton in this election. Voters who usually vote Republican but can't bring themselves to pull the lever for Trump may decide to stay home. Turnout is unpredictable, and the effect of low voter turnout is also unpredictable.

So for all these reasons and others, no one can tell how this election will turn out. It will be a tragedy and an insult to democracy if the election were to be decided by those who fail to vote, rather than by those who come out to vote for or against one of the two major candidates. So even if you are not aroused by either Clinton or Trump in this most critical of elections, vote for the one who would be better than the other. Or vote against the one who would be worse. But vote.

Acknowledgments

This book could not have been written as quickly without the valuable assistance of my research team, Aaron Voloj Dessauer and Nicholas Maisel, who researched and contributed to the text and footnotes, and my assistants Maura Kelley, who deciphered and typed my handwritten drafts, and Sarah Neely, who provided her usual invaluable assistance. You all know how much I appreciate your extraordinary efforts. A special thanks to my new agent, Karen Gantz, who made this book happen and guided me through the process.

My appreciation as well to my wife, Carolyn Cohen, who reads, reviews, and corrects everything I write, and to Alan Rothfeld, Michael Miller, Tom Ashe, Harvey Silverglate, Elon Dershowitz, Jamin Dershowitz, Ella Dershowitz, and others who critiqued my words.

It takes a village to write a book, and my summer village, where I wrote this book, is largely on Martha's Vineyard, most particularly, on the porch of the Chilmark Store, where everything I write and say is put to the test of both humor and serious critique.

Notes

Introduction

1. Lisa Lerer and Emily Swanson, "Fear Factor: Americans Scared of Their Presidential Options," *AP, The Big Story*, July 14, 2016.
2. Lela Moore and Michelle Baruchman, "I'm Resigned to Having a Terrible President," *New York Times*, July 30, 2016.
3. Yaron Steinbuch, "Most Americans Are Scared of Clinton or Trump as President," *New York Post*, July 14, 2016, citing AP-GFK poll.
4. Gallup poll, "Congressional Job Approval Ratings Trend, 1974–present," http://www.gallup.com/poll/1600/congress-public.aspx.
5. Andrea Park, "Susan Sarandon Slams Campaign Against Bernie Sanders While Attending the DNC," People.com, July 26, 2016.
6. "Susan Sarandon at the Democratic National Convention: The Climate Revolution Continues," *Democracy Now*, July 25, 2016.
7. Chris Mejaski, "Susan Sarandon Agrees: She's Having the 'Worst Time' at the Democratic National Convention," Etalk.ca, July 26, 2016.
8. Kevin Baker, "Let's Grow Up, Liberals," *New York Times*, July 13, 2016.

1: The Causes of the Dysfunction

1. Neil Genzlinger, "Review: 'Can We Take a Joke?' The Answer Appears to Be Not Anymore," *New York Times*, July 28, 2016.
2. Roger Nash Baldwin, "Traveling Hopefully," in *Liberties Lost: The Endangered Legacy of the ACLU* (Westport, Conn.: Greenwood Publishing Group, 2006), p. 113.
3. John Stuart Mill, *On Liberty*, quoted in Alan M. Dershowitz, *Shouting Fire* (New York: Little, Brown and Company, 2002), p. 134.
4. Alan M. Dershowitz, "Whom Do Bigots Blame for Police Shootings in America? Israel, Of Course!" *Jerusalem Post*, July 14, 2016.
5. To better understand the term "pinkwashing" in the context of Israel, see Sarah Schulman, "Israel and Pinkwashing," *New York Times*, November 22, 2011.
6. "Haaretz Writer Booted from Palestinian School Because She's Israeli Jew," *Times of Israel*, September 28, 2014.
7. Kristian Davis Bailey & Khury Petersen-Smith, "1,000 Black Activists, Artists, and Scholars Demand Justice for Palestine," *Ebony*, August 18, 2015.
8. Julie Zauzmer, "Jewish Groups Decry Black Lives Matter Platform's

Views on Israel," *Washington Post*, August 5, 2016.

9. "Dr. Cornel West today at the #MASSIVE rally and March in #CLE #BlackLivesMatter," YouTube video, 9:41, posted by "SVS Mediaworks," July 16, 2016, https://www.youtube.com/watch?v=o2G-hyauZj8.

10. "Watch Hillary Clinton's full speech at the 2016 Democratic National Convention," YouTube video, 1:05:23, from a broadcast on PBS *NewsHour* on July 28, 2016, posted by "PBS NewsHour," July 28, 2016, https://www.youtube.com/watch?v=pnXiy4D_I8g?t=46m.

11. See, e.g., "Has Obama Turned on Israel," *Wall Street Journal*, July 3, 2009; "Obama's Legacy and the Iranian Bomb," *Wall Street Journal*, March 23, 2010; "The Appalling Talk of Boycotting Netanyahu," *Wall Street Journal*, February 23, 2015; "Hold Iran to the Language in the Deal," *Wall Street Journal*, September 7, 2015. These op-eds were reprinted in my book *The Case Against the Iran Deal* (New York: RosettaBooks, 2015).

12. Mark Landler, "How Hillary Clinton Became a Hawk," *New York Times Magazine*, April 21, 2016.

13. Alan M. Dershowitz, "President Obama Turns a Corner on Iran," *Algemeiner*, March 2, 2012.

2: The Virtues and Vices of Unchecked Populism

1. Tamara Keith, "Has Bernie Sanders Moved Hillary Clinton to the Left?" *NPR Morning Edition*, March 31, 2016.

2. For more information, see "Bernie Sanders: On the Issues," Bernie Sanders's 2016 campaign website, accessed August 8, 2016, https://berniesanders.com/issues/.

3. Danielle Kurtzleben, "Study: Sanders' Proposals Would Add $18 Trillion to Debt Over the Next 10 Years," *NPR*, May 9, 2016.

4. "Donald Trump's Budget Plan Would Add $10 Trillion in Debt," *AP*, June 27, 2016.

5. Jeffrey Lazarus, "Hillary Clinton Was a More Effective Lawmaker Than Bernie Sanders," *Washington Post*, April 7, 2016.

6. Amanda Marcotte, "Trump and Brexit: Right-wing Populism of the Two Is Rooted More in Base Nationalism Than in Economic Insecurity," *Salon*, June 24, 2016.

7. James Madison, Federalist No. 10: "The Same Subject Continued: The Union as a Safeguard Against Domestic Faction and Insurrection." *New York Daily Advertiser*, November 22, 1787.

8. Charles Callan Tansill, "Notes of the Secret Debates of the Federal Convention of 1787, Taken by the Late Hon Robert Yates," *Documents Illustrative of the Formation of the Union of the American States* (Washington: Government Printing Office, 1927).

9. Ibid.

10. Bernard Henri-Lévy, "The United Kingdom's Strange Defeat," *The Huffington Post*, June 27, 2016.

11. Alexis de Tocqueville, *Democracy in America*, trans. Henry Reeve (New York: Edward Walker, 1847).

12. Ibid.

13. Nonna Gorilovskaya, "The Dissident: An Interview With Natan Sharansky," *Mother Jones*, March 30, 2005.

14. Will Marshall, "The GOP Clown Show," *Daily Beast*, July 17, 2016.

15. Mark Memmott, "Calling Obamacare 'Fascism' Was 'Poor Choice of Words,' Whole Foods CEO Says," *NPR*, January 17, 2013.

16. Trump: "If I told the real stories of my experiences with women, often seemingly very happily married and important women, this book would be a guaranteed best-seller." From *The Art of the Comeback*, cited by Carlos Lozada, "Donald Trump on women, sex, marriage, and feminism," *Washington Post*, August 5, 2015.

17. "President Obama's Speech at the Democratic Convention," *Washington Post*, July 28, 2016.

18. See, for example, "Only Jobbik Satisfied as Fidesz Marches On," *Budapest Times*, October 17, 2014, and "Local Elections—Orban: 'Third Win' in the Bag Amid Low Turnout," *Daily News Hungary*, October 13, 2014.

19. Associated Press, "Hungarian Leader, Viktor Orban, Says Donald Trump is Better for Europe," *New York Times*, July 23, 2016, http://www.nytimes.com/2016/07/24/world/americas/hungarys-vikto r-orban-says-donald-trump-is-better-for-europe.html.

20. "Controversial Monument Divides Hungarians, Angers Jewish Community," EurActiv.com, July 23, 2014.

21. Bernard Rorke, "Hungary's Fidesz and Its 'Jewish Question,'" openDemocracy.net, September 22, 2014.

22. Alan Dershowitz, "Europe's Old (and New) Hells Remind Us of Israel's Importance," Fox News, May 16, 2016.

23. Anna Sauerbrey, "Germany's Violent Extremes," *New York Times*, July 28, 2016.

24. Ronald Radosh, "Bernie's Campaign Invites a Leader of a Spanish Anti-Semitic and Anti-Israel Group to the Democratic Convention," Hudson.org, July 24, 2016.

25. "The right attacks immigrants while the left rails at bankers, but the spirit of insurgency, the venting of anger at those in power, and the addiction to simple demagogic answers to complex problems are the same for both extremes." Tony Blair, "Brexit's Stunning Coup," *New*

York Times, June 24, 2016.

26. Ibid.

27. Paul Krugman, "Delusions of Chaos," *New York Times*, July 25, 2016.

28. Newt Gingrich, quoted in Matthew Gault, "Donald Trump Has Americanized Vladimir Putin's War on Truth," *The Week*, August 4, 2016.

29. Ibid.

30. Cass R. Sunstein, "How Facebook Makes Us Dumber," *Bloomberg View*, January 8, 2016.

31. "Bill Clinton: The World Is Coming Apart on President Obama," YouTube video, 0:23, from a broadcast on ABC News, posted by "Howard Griffin," April 7, 2016, https://www.youtube.com/watch?v=ZhiheluICWs.

32. Michael Barbaro and Alexander Burns, "It's Donald Trump's Convention. But the Inspiration? Nixon." *New York Times*, July 18, 2016.

33. Tara Golshan, "Hillary Clinton's victory speech: 'Don't let anyone tell you that great things can't happen." *Vox*, June 8, 2016.

3: The Case Against Democracy by Default

1. Ajamu Baraka, "Sanctions for Russia and a Green Light for Israel to Continue War Crimes," *Common Dreams*, August 2, 2014. See also, Ajamu Baraka, "Witness to an International Crime: Israeli State Terrorism in Gaza," *Black Agenda Report*, July 15, 2014.

2. Nathan Guttman, "5 Questions for Tim Kaine on Israel," *Forward*, March 13, 2015.

3. Ali Vitali, "Donald Trump on Terror: 'You Have to Fight Fire With Fire," NBC News, June 29, 2016.

4. Haeyoon Park, "Trump Vows to Stop Immigration From Nations 'Compromised' by Terrorism. How Could It Work?" *New York Times*, July 22, 2016.

5. Joseph Goldstein, "Defeat of ISIS Could Send 'Terrorist Diaspora' to West, F.B.I. Chief Says," *New York Times*, July 27, 2016.

6. Peter Baker, "Syria Exposes Split Between Obama and Clinton," *New York Times*, October 3, 2015.

7. Sixth Republican debate, January 14, 2016. Transcript available at https://www.washingtonpost.com/news/the-fix/wp/2016/01/14/6th-republican-debate-transcript-annotated-who-said-what-and-what-it-meant/.

8. Rosalind S. Helderman, "Here's What We Know About Donald Trump And His Ties to Russia," *The Washington Post*, July 29, 2016.

9. Jeremy Diamond, "Donald Trump's 'Star of David' Tweet Controversy, Explained" *CNN*, July 5, 2016.

10. Trump had in fact disavowed David Duke on numerous prior occasions before he began his run for president in 2015. Eric Bradner, "Donald Trump Stumbles on David Duke, KKK," *CNN*, February 29, 2016.

11. Most memorably, Trump told audience members, "I'm a negotiator, like you folks…. Is there anyone in this room who doesn't negotiate deals? … Probably more than any room I've ever spoken." Patricia Mazzei and Lesley Clark, "Donald Trump Stereotypes Jews in Speech to Republican Jewish Coalition," *The Miami Herald*, December 3, 2015.

12. David Friedman, interview by Ynetnews, "Interview with Trump's Israel Advisor, a Jew Who 'Truly Loves Israel,'" April 8, 2016, http://www.ynetnews.com/articles/0,7340,L-4837669,00.html.

13. David Leonhardt, "The Clear and Present Danger of Donald Trump," *New York Times*, July 28, 2016.

14. Molly Redden, "Clinton Leads Way on Abortion Rights as Democrats Seek End to Decades-Old Rule," *Guardian*, July 26, 2016.

15. Hillary Clinton, "Remarks at the Opening Plenary of the US-Morocco Strategic Dialogue," (address, US Department of State, Washington, DC, September 13, 2012).

16. Mark Joseph Stern, "Of Course Donald Trump Is the Most Pro-Gay Republican Presidential Candidate," *Slate*, December 18, 2015.

17. S. E. Cupp, "Trump Is Right on Transgender Bathroom Laws," CNN. com, April 25, 2016.

18. Bradford Richardson, "Donald Trump Backtracks on Transgender Bathroom Issue," *Washington Times*, April 22, 2016.

19. "FULL Donald Trump Town Hall With Chris Matthews [Part 3] - March 30th 2016 | FIERY ABORTION SEGMENT!," YouTube video, 14:56, from a broadcast on MSNBC, posted by "Election News," March 30, 2016, https://www.youtube.com/watch?v=aUClmJN4HhI.

20. See David Sherfinksi, "Donald Trump: 'To the Best of My Knowledge,' Not Too Many Evangelicals Come Out Of Cuba," *Washington Times*, December 30, 2015.

21. Emily Flitter and Steve Holland, "Trump Preparing Plan to Dismantle Obama's Wall Street Reform Law," Reuters, May 18, 2016.

22. Jeremy Diamond and Stephen Collinson, "Donald Trump: 'Second Amendment' Gun Advocates Should Deal with Hillary Clinton," *CNN*, August 10, 2016.

23. John Daniel Davidson, "The Second Amendment Isn't About Hunting or Self-Defense, But Revolution," *The Federalist*, June 20, 2016.

24. For a literature review on this issue, see Lisa Hepburn and David Hemenway, "Firearm Availability and Homicide: A Review of the Literature," *Aggression and Violent Behavior* 9, no. 4 (July 2004): 417–440.

25. Jeremy Diamond, "Donald Trump: Ban All Muslim Travel to U.S." *CNN*, December 8, 2015.

26. Michelle Ye Hee Lee, "Donald Trump Flip-Flops, Then Flips and Flops More on H-1B Visas," *Washington Post*, March 21, 2016.

Conclusion

1. See, for example, Bloomberg's Brexit watch at http://www.bloomberg.com/graphics/2016-brexit-watch/.

2. Eshe Nelson, Chiara Albanese, and Lyubov Pronina, "How They Got It So Wrong. Complacent Traders Stunned by Brexit," Bloomberg Markets, June 24, 2016.

3. Christina Wilkie, "Trump On Second Amendment Backlash: 'I Think It's A Good Thing For Me,'" *Huffington Post*, August 10, 2016.

4. Brent Sadler, "Suicide Bombings Scar Peres's Political Ambitions," CNN, May 28, 1996.

CPSIA information can be obtained at www.ICGtesting.com
Printed in the USA
LVOW09*0156300816

502327LV00015BA/182/P